2500

DEFYING DISAFFECTION
how schools are winning the hearts
and minds of reluctant students

7

DEFYING DISAFFECTION

how schools are winning the hearts and minds of reluctant students

Reva Klein

Trentham Books

First published in 1999 by Trentham Books Limited
Reprinted in 2000

Trentham Books Limited
Westview House
734 London Road
Oakhill
Stoke on Trent
Staffordshire
England ST4 5NP

British Cataloguing in Publication Data
A catalogue record for this book is available from the British Library

ISBN 1 85856 162 0 (pb)
ISBN 1 85856 161 2 (hb)

Designed and typeset by Trentham Print Design Ltd., Chester and printed in Great Britain by Professional Book Supplies Ltd., Oxford

Contents

Acknowledgements

I consider myself privileged. As a journalist and a writer, I've travelled around Britain, America and elsewhere meeting hundreds of teachers, headteachers, pupils, parents, people working in voluntary organisations and academics who have opened their lives, work and often their hearts to me.

Through them, I've seen more humanity, hope, inspiration and old-fashioned goodness than I could have hoped to find anywhere else. On both sides of the Atlantic I've been moved to my roots by teachers who pour their energies into kids whom others have written off as irredeemable, who have devoted their lives – holidays and weekends, too – to making things better for the children in their care. I've been humbled, too, by children and young people who despite abuse, poverty and hopelessness at home, have retained their dignity and desire to learn. To all of them, I pay homage and owe many, many thanks.

By concentrating on American models of innovative practice in this book, I'm in no way inferring that there isn't outstanding work with disaffected children going on in many places in the UK. There is and I've been fortunate enough to see some of it for myself and document it elsewhere. But I have chosen to look to the US because the programmes there are by and large more established, have been assessed, enjoy a firmer funding base and, most importantly, tend to be radical in approach.

I'm particularly grateful to the following for their generosity in time and ideas: Marty Duckenfield and Dr Jay Smink of the National Dropout Prevention Center in South Carolina, John D'Abbro, headteacher of New Rush Hall EBD School in Redbridge and Terry Emerson at NRH Annex, Peter Evans at the OECD, Paris and staff at Jefferson County High School, Hostos Lincoln Academy, Communities in Schools, Palm Beach County and TOP in Roanoke. I'm also thankful to all the young people I met in these places who have told me their stories with so much honesty and candour.

I also want to thank Caroline St John Brooks, Angela Phillips, Judy Larsen and Rob Smith for kindly reading the manuscript and giving such useful feedback; Angela and Jan McKenley for encouraging me to embark on this book and counselling me through my moments in the wilderness; David Budge for heaping mounds of resources and contacts at my feet; Daniel Goleman for his time and generosity.

And Dave Veltman, whose calmness and cajolery in the face of adversity is truly superhuman.

And last but not least, to Gillian Klein, my editor and publisher, more thanks than I can express for her enthusiasm, warmth, good humour and belief in me.

DEDICATION

To the long-suffering but wonderfully resilient Jodie and Max, whose laughter and love have seen me through the agonies, the ecstasies and all the bits in between, and will continue to do so forever.

FOREWORD

Disaffection is a worldwide problem. Few schools are relevant to every student within their walls. It's not hard, wherever you look, to find children who can't connect with teachers or with what is being taught, or who feel like outsiders – for whatever reason. Likewise, its not hard to find headteachers and class teachers who fail to identify or deal appropriately with those problems or know where to turn for help – again, for whatever reason.

But the good news is that there are pockets of success, schools where there is a commitment on the part of the entire school community, as well as the local community and business leaders, to get all students on board achieving, enjoying themselves and having aspirations. These are schools that acknowledge a simple truth: they can't do it on their own. They have discovered that it doesn't take a lot of money to embrace social inclusion, but it does require determination and persistence, the willingness to listen and learn from others and the courage to take routes that may not have been taken before to achieve their aims.

In *Defying Disaffection*, Reva Klein has combined the research skills of an accomplished journalist, the eloquence of a polished writer and the passion of an advocate for youth to describe the realities of the school dropout issue in the United States and in the UK. Fuelled by her own experience of alienation in a high school like so many others – not bad but impervious to the problems and needs of its students – she has identified the very best ideas and practice of dropout prevention in its myriad forms, describing them with rigor, colour and warmth.

A *leitmotif* of the book is the belief that prevention is better than cure. A comprehensive programme of encouraging learning, emotional literacy and communication that begins in the pre-school years is the most intelligent, holistic and long-term approach to successful learning and social competency. But on the other side of the equation, schools must be sympathetic to this approach and follow it through, respecting and addressing children's individuality and different ways of learning, their rights to express themselves, their need for inter-active learning, and their emotional and social needs. If schools remain stuck in the ways of the past, they will subvert all the good work that is beginning to take hold at pre-school level. Schools must be part of a supportive continuum that begins at the earliest stages, not a law unto themselves.

This book offers perspectives on how schools can achieve this. Re-inventing wheels to make political mileage, as the author points out, is a cynical and wasteful exercise. In these pages, there are approaches to social inclusion in schools that can be mixed and matched or cloned or reworked to help alleviate the student disengagement that beleaguers so many schools in the developed world. What they repre-sent is not only an improvement in the learning opportunities and daily lives of youth in our schools, but an improvement in the spirit of schools as a whole. Central to that spirit, of course, is the satisfaction teachers derive from knowing that they have made a difference to reluctant students' lives.

The highly readable research, information and insights presented in this book make it a must-read for all educators, policymakers and community leaders on both sides of the Atlantic. It is an important book for everyone who believes that school dropout and disaffection are not only avoidable, but also that they can and must be eradicated if our societies are to be equipped to meet the challenges of the 21st century.

Dr Jay Smink
Executive Director
National Dropout Prevention Center
Clemson, South Carolina

INTRODUCTION

There's Something Rotten in the
State of Education

Disaffection is not an abstract concept to me. I have first-hand knowledge of it. In the late 1960s in the American midwest, I was a textbook example of what Americans call an at-risk student, someone at risk of dropping out. Truancy, underachievement, disruptive behaviour, drug abuse – I had all the hallmarks of a typically poor, inner-city kid struggling to survive. Except that I wasn't. Brought up in a traditional, white middle class home in the suburbs, on the surface I had a lot going for me. But what I didn't have was a foothold in an education system that though not overly rigid was highly structured; not massively huge but big enough to lose sight of the individuals within it; not unusually traditional but sufficiently out of step with the spirit of the times to feel like an alien, dissociated world to the alienated, dissociated teenager I'd become. And although I didn't have a problematic background compared to many, I had enough darkness in my life to make me desperate for attention, direction and compassion, leading me to act out in self-destructive ways.

If it hadn't been for the sensitivity, insight and superhuman patience of one of my teachers, I don't know what my fate would have been. While other teachers gave up on me when it became clear that I'd given up on them, my journalism teacher took the trouble to look beyond my dilated pupils and sense that there was someone in there desperate to achieve at something of real, three dimensional value. So where others retreated from me in a mirror image of my retreat from them, she came closer, giving me more and more responsibilities, challenges and status. Her expectations were high and it was her belief in my ability to meet those expectations in the end that motivated me to not only hang in there, but to shine.

Although I was singularly lucky to have a teacher like Barbara Abbott, I wasn't alone in having trouble fitting in. There were peers of similar socio-economic background as well as some from seriously rich families who fit the description of maladjusted. Their parents stood back in betrayed disbelief as these kids who had everything that 1960s America could offer – freedom and money – rejected it all, including an education that they saw as irrelevant in content and bureaucratic in delivery.

There were others, too, black and white, who came from poorer families or troubled households. Their rejection of school was borne of alienation from a white, middle class, sports dominated, wealth obsessed school culture that was far removed from everything they knew. What had physics and geometry to do with being a second class citizen, living in a suburban ghetto, being valued only for your athletic prowess or your ability to act the clown when the situation demanded it? The social apartheid that the world has had a glimmer of through the horrific massacre at Columbine High School near Denver, where two students killed twelve classmates and a teacher before turning guns on themselves, has a long history in American schools. My school was part of the tradition that led those two boys to become so alienated and resentful.

But disaffection isn't unique to America; nor is it always a result of social divisiveness. It's wider and more complex. Disaffection in schools is endemic in American and British society. You'll find it wherever there are institutions called schools and children who are required by law to attend them. It is expressed and defined as persistent truancy, disruptive behaviour, alienation and withdrawal or any combination of these. Often but not always, it is associated with underachievement. However it is played out, it is not a new phenomenon. It has probably been around since schools began. But the situation is worsening as schools are becoming more goal-oriented and less flexible and, as part and parcel of those changes, increasingly unwilling to accommodate diversity of behaviour, cultural expression and ways of learning.

The irony is that this narrowing approach to education comes at a time when the notion of social inclusion in schools has never been greater on both sides of the Atlantic. The view that the majority of children can and should be accommodated in mainstream schools has as much political currency today as racial integration had in the United States in the 1960s and 1970s. It is seen as a basic human right.

But there are cautionary lessons for inclusionists to learn from the desegregationists. We have watched racial integration in the United States delivered after a long, bloody labour and, over three decades, die a slow, tortuous death in many sectors of American society. While the legislation exists to uphold individuals' rights to live and go to school where they choose, blacks and whites on the whole choose not to live and go to school together. The laws may have changed, but the attitudes, by and large, haven't. And without seismic shifts in attitude, racial integration is superficial.

So we may find in the sphere of social inclusion in schools. We have policies today that support the principle of all children being educated under the same roof irrespective of their physical, cognitive and emotional differences. But, like racial integration, these policies are destined to meet an untimely end unless they bring with them a sea change in attitude, a redefinition of education and a restructuring of our schools.

This book is about how schools can transform themselves so that the disaffected, the disenfranchised, the demoralised and the educationally disoriented can come to feel part of their schools and flourish within them. And it is about how some schools and programmes in the United States have managed to turn students' lives around by using radical, unconventional and even risky approaches as part of their transformations. They are schools in which the disaffected are not only learning and graduating, but where they are being given back their futures against all conceivable odds.

Most of all, this book is an impassioned call for educationalists and policy makers to grasp the nettle and look creatively at the problem and boldly at the options. If yet another generation of young people – the proverbial square pegs who don't fit into the round holes of education systems – are not to be lost, we need to be thinking and acting now. In Britain sweeping reforms such as education action zones and blueprints for tackling disaffection among young people are coming out out thick and fast from the Social Exclusion Unit and the Department for Education and Employment and New Labour, in power since May 1997, is ostensibly responsive to new thinking and new practices.

The time for palliatives is over. We don't need more Pupil Referral Units: we need to rethink the whole process that leads children to winding up in PRUs in the first place. We don't need punishments heaped on schools that exclude students because they don't have the resources or expertise to deal with them: we need to ensure that all schools are able to accommodate these young people by creating structures that are more pupil-friendly and a curriculum that is more engaging. And we need to look at how to support those pupils to prevent them from dropping out with their minds and spirits, before they take their bodies with them out the door. If New Labour is about joined up thinking, then the problems that afflict children and young people in our schools have to be reviewed, analysed and addressed holistically, collaboratively, from the bottom up. Prevention is so much better than cure.

But why focus on America of all places? Good question. Public education in the US is a total anomaly: inspiring and depressing, stimulating and stultifying, progressive and backward. It encompasses some of the worst schools in the western world and some of the best. At its most dire, it produces dropout statistics, poor attainment, illiteracy and innumeracy that leave other countries reeling in disbelief. At its best, it is willing to look its problems in the face and think laterally in the search for creative ways of tackling them. The schools and programmes I've chosen to look at will be illustrating some dynamic thinking and some staggeringly good outcomes.

As Mary Warnock highlighted in her watershed 1978 report on special educational needs that heralded the road to inclusion, every child has its own unique needs. Some, like mine, will have a psychological or emotional base. For others, they will be cognitive. For many others, their most pressing problems will result from the socio-economic circumstances in which they live. In the coming chapters, I'll be looking at the myriad risk factors of disaffection.

In education, it always takes two to tango. Schools and the teachers in them are never the sole causes of disaffection. There is always baggage that a child brings into school that predisposes them to problems fitting in. This can happen in the best and most caring of schools. But it's more likely to grow into a bigger problem when the structures are inflexible and the climate depersonalised. Because children spend upwards of six hours a day in school, it is an environment that can make or break the child who is labouring under difficulties. Schools have the potential to offer either support and nurturing or an alienating climate that says 'we don't want you.' Because of this, when it comes to disaffection, we have to look at the object of the disaffection to make sense of the problem and lead us to solutions.

There are many contributing factors within the four walls of any school that can tip the unresilient, at-risk child over the edge and into the quagmire of disaffection. The one-dimensionally goal-oriented culture that many schools have bought into since the British education reforms of the late 1980s have worked against children who have different learning styles or children whose social, emotional and behavioral problems stand in the way of their cognitive abilities. Far from the agenda being set by an entitlement curriculum that gives all children an equal chance, there is growing evidence that schools are concentrating their energies more on the children likely to do well in exams than on children who look set to do poorly. In further chapters, I'll be looking at how these reforms have led to a narrow, competitive vision of education that sees differentness as a problem and a problem as something that is unwanted – and at how those 'problematic' children can so easily drift into alienation.

One aspect of the increasingly achievement-driven school culture is the reintroduction of setting, starting at primary level. This trend is accelerating despite a substantial body of evidence showing that homogeneous grouping (various types of grouping by ability, including setting and streaming – called tracking in the US) can be harmful to certain groups of pupils. According to an NFER report, grouping by ability 'has a negative impact on the achievement and schooling experiences of pupils of low ability and those who belong to particular social groups' (for example, pupils from working-class and ethnic minority backgrounds, boys and summer-born children.) There is also the suggestion that some pupils, no matter what their ability, may find such grouping stressful.

The report cites the main disadvantages: that setting ignores the fact that pupils' rates and styles of learning differ, no matter what their level of ability; that progress made by pupils in top sets is offset by the lack of progress made by lower ability pupils; that grouping by ability underlines the differences between pupils and discriminates against certain groups (see above) and reinforces negative stereotypes; and that the focus on high ranking in the league tables has led to the sidelining of emotional and social development in favour of the acquisition of knowledge.[1]

An excessively punitive response to disciplinary problems is another contributing factor to pupil disaffection. Many young people who have been excluded or have drifted away from school complain of having been unfairly dealt with at school by teachers who were 'out to get' them. While there are always two sides to any story and while children are all too capable of presenting themselves as innocent victims when they're anything but, we have to listen to them. In view of the rising exclusion rates over the past decade, what seems clear is that the tolerance level of some schools has lowered to the point where even minor infractions are exacting a heavy price.

Then there's the question of content and pedagogy. Much has been written about how a curriculum that bears no relation to children's experiences, talents and interests can be a major deterrent to motivation. And all teachers will know that lessons that are wholly conceptual rather than differentiated in teaching style, teacher dominated rather than interactive, aimed at one level rather than varying levels, are unlikely to engage pupils. Eurocentricity, too, exacts a heavy price. Toni Morrison puts its consequences like this: 'Certain absences are so stressed, are so ornate, so planned, they call attention to themselves: arrest us with intentionality and purpose like neighbourhoods that are defined by the population held away from them.'[2]

The positive side of all this is that while the diverse social and economic factors working against children are notoriously difficult to shift, there are achievable alternatives to the factors that make schools untenable for at-risk students. Take one of the most important and obvious factors in children's sense of engagement with school: size. While small schools, as every on-message local authority and Department for Education bureaucrat worth their salt will tell you, are not cost effective, there are structures that can be put in place to mitigate the alienation that comes from being in large classes within large schools. The ideal is to reduce class size. But since that option is increasingly difficult as good state schools are oversubscribed and bursting at the seams, there is another alternative: the creation of small family groups within each year group that meet together at one or two key points in the day to 'debrief' with the same teacher year in, year out. The teacher gets to know the students and the students bond with each other and with the teacher, creating a safe sense of micro community within the larger institution. This takes conventional tutor groups a stage further, transforming them into nurturing sanctuaries of openness and informality, led by teachers who have undergone in-service training in social and emotional development and counselling skills.

Just as central as size is school ethos. Walk into a school where teachers are locked in a 'them and us' mindset, where students are seen as either good or bad, where race, class and cultural background are perceived as the defining features of children and where respect, patience and tolerance are considered privileges to be won rather than the right of every student and you'll find a school in which children are disengaged, underachieving and resentful. It will be a school where conflict between staff and children is replicated among children and where children do not feel safe and secure. It will be a school where staff themselves are disaffected, bad-tempered, unfulfilled. I've visited such schools, thankfully very few but totally unforgettable, where the negativity is palpable in the air from the minute you walk through the door. Teachers who don't smile, who make little direct eye contact, whose voices have the tone of drill sergeants, who react to every inter-action as if it were a problem, where even in the staffroom an uneasy silence sets you on edge. Unhappy people in unhappy, mismanaged schools.

Then go to a school that recognises and values the individual and gives children a democratic voice. You find that this positive ethos is com-municated in everything from the tone and content of interpersonal exchanges between student and teacher to the way progress, no matter how small, is acknowledged; and from how staff deal with behaviour problems and emotional eruptions to the way they encourage co-operation inside as well as outside the classroom. Humanity in a school, from headteacher to lunchtime supervisors, from classroom teachers to governors, should be as integral to a school as bricks and mortar. Children treated with sarcasm, derision or indifference are unlikely to feel good about themselves or their teachers and will take their uneasy feelings around with them, in their work, in the dinner hall, in the playground and out onto the streets. They will also be less inclined to want to put themselves out academically for such teachers. Children who know they are valued and are given the help they need to reach their potential will carry with them self-respect as well as respect for teachers and the learning process.

Teaching methodology, too, is crucial. Teaching staff require not only training in aspects of the curriculum and behaviour management but a real understanding of the importance of differentiated teaching to encompass the gamut of abilities and learning styles that exist within any one classroom. Acknowledging differences in styles and abilities doesn't mean pitching work at the lowest common denominator. It means presenting work that is challenging at a level that is realistic and providing appropriate support. With this must come assessment that not only reflects students' progress but also encourages and supports them to build on their achievements consistently.

Central to the issue of disaffection is a reassessment of that most unloved and marginalised of subjects, Personal, Social and Health Education. While PSHE has the potential to re-engage disaffected students, as the House of Commons Education and Employment Committee's report on disaffected children points out, too much of it is being delivered badly, is poorly conceived and amounts to little more than 'high-handed waffle.'[3]

What it requires is rigour. That this can be achieved, now that the National Curriculum Review has kept PSHE outside statutory requirements, seems doubtful. That this was a wasted opportunity for raising its profile and status is beyond doubt. Ask any of the furious and disappointed teachers who believe in the power of PSHE to encourage self-awareness, heighten self-esteem and shift young people's attitudes towards school, relationships and their futures

A good school that is as concerned with the psychological well-being of its pupils as with their SATs results will, despite the scheduling obstacles, work towards building up and developing PSHE as a curricular area that facilitates inclusion as well as being a vehicle for delivering important social, emotional and life management skills in dynamic and interactive ways. The crucial proviso is that it must be taught by teachers who are properly trained and committed to it.

Communication with parents is another essential part of schools' battle against disaffection. Without parents and the wider community on board, the humane school environment that is comfortable with diversity, that is truly socially inclusive and supports achievement and the striving for it, can't hope to survive outside its four walls. Parents, not schools, exert the strongest influence on children. If attitudes to and within schools are to change, parents must be communicated with in ways that engage them and meet their needs, too. Teachers must realise that parents are often distrustful towards them because of their own negative experiences as children. They must also confront the fact that parents don't exist solely as the receptacles for bad news about their children's problem behaviour or poor attainment. If they are to be won over to the value of their children's education and the important role that they have to play, they must be offered positive overtures and given encouraging glimpses of their children, too.

The rhetoric about parents becoming partners in educating their children must move on to address how the very real barriers between school and home can be broken down for everyone's benefit. Offering biscuits at parents' evenings where ten minutes per child is allocated, if you're lucky, isn't enough. New channels, however difficult, must be opened up. One way is by allowing parents to experience their children as learners and even as teachers through regular parent/pupil workshops on computers or crafts, for instance. When parents see that their children's learning has a life outside the classroom, when their skills and knowledge are presented as having practical applications, parents disengaged with their children's schooling begin to look at things differently. Another way is by giving parents different ways in to the school, by offering courses that enhance their own knowledge and employability and perhaps allow them to use their new skills in the school.

As no man or woman, boy or girl is an island, neither is any school. Under-resourcing, curricular pressures, inadequate training and low morale among staff help to militate against creating the content and climate for social inclusion in schools without outside help. A collaboration between statutory agencies and community-based voluntary organisations can bring massive amounts of needed expertise and different strategies into schools to motivate children and focus on self-esteem and social skills. Mentoring, social work, counselling and community service projects are all examples of how outside agencies can contribute to schools' attempts to address students' pressing problems. Bringing the outside world and schools closer together benefits everybody.

For hard-pressed schools with their backs against the wall, making structural changes that answer the needs of all students is a tall order, with major ramifications for the national curriculum as well as for teacher training, local authority/school district support, school management and whole school policies. What it requires is a process involving no less than a re-examination of educational priorities and a head-on, honest look at inclusiveness. Reverting to the bad old days of channelling the 'unacademic' or disruptive pupils into vocational studies or segregated units from which they never emerge is socially divisive, discriminatory and no longer relevant. It's time we looked at our mistakes. It's time to creatively bring together best practice from wherever it's found – from around Britain, from the rest of Europe, from the United States and from Australia – in a coordinated, intelligent and humane fashion, underpinned with a broad view of what children need for the 2000s.

References

1. Sikhnandan, L. and Lee, B. *Streaming, Setting and Grouping by Ability*, National Foundation for Educational Research, 1998.
2. Morrison, T. Unspeakable Things Unspoken: The African-American presence in American Literature, *Michigan Quarterly*, Volume 28, 1989.
3. House of Commons Education and Employment Committee, Fifth Report Volume I, London: The Stationery Office, April 1, 1998.

A note for American readers.

LEA – Local Education Authority, roughly parallel to school districts. Their powers over schools have been severely diminished over the past decade.

EBD – Emotional and behaviour difficulties.

PRU – Pupil referral unit, a smaller scale version of alternative high schools.

DfEE – Department for Education and Employment, the government ministry that legislates education practice, content and policy.

CHAPTER ONE

WHO ARE THESE KIDS?

We gotta get outta this place
If it's the last thing we ever do...
The Animals

We all think we know the young and disaffected when we see them in school or on the streets. It's in their gestures and the way they move, in the way they avoid looking you in the eye and in their monosyllabic speech. It's in the way they take pains to demonstrate to teachers and peers that they're bored and unconcerned with what's going on around them by being late, by not participating or cooperating, by being rude or withdrawn or a combination of all these things. It's in the way they don't show up or are there one minute and gone the next. It's in the way that, whatever they do, they have the uncanny knack of drawing negative attention to themselves – or, alternatively, of making themselves invisible.

In *Three to Remember: Strategies for Disaffected Pupils*,[1] Kinder *et al* refer to the three main factors of disaffection: 'individual pathologies or personality traits; family circumstances or values and/or social factors within the non-attenders' communities; and school factors, often located in either the curriculum or the ethos and relationships encountered there by pupils'. I would add to this list the social constructions of problematic children with specific reference to race, class and gender. Clearly, the factors often overlap.

The authors point out that given the often intractable problems children face, the impact that schools or local education authorities can make on them will be variable. It is certainly true that some of the problems that lead the young to become disengaged are intractable. The figures correlating poverty with poor academic outcomes speak for themselves. In

Britain, one child in three lives in a family earning less than half the average income. While GCSE results have steadily risen during the 1990s, there are still 220,000 young people in the UK who have not obtained anything above a grade D, most of them from poor families. Between 1987 and 1996, the number of pupils from unskilled family backgrounds achieving at least five A-C GCSEs rose by eight percentage points to 19% while those from professional families leapt by 18 percentage points to 77%.[2]

A Canadian study puts it succinctly: 'The lower the occupational status and level of education of his/her parents, the greater is the statistical risk that any given student will not complete school'.[3] To put it in another context, the US Educational Testing Service reports that around half of all families on welfare (social security) in the United States are headed by early school leavers.[4]

Additional family experiences have similarly critical influences on drop-out rates. Another Canadian study, admittedly a small one, of twelve young male offenders who had all dropped out of high school showed that approximately two thirds had experienced some level of child abuse. In addition, they had had an average of ten household moves and a large proportion reported a history of family crisis intervention, ie, children being taken into care. Half the young men's parents were regular substance abusers and eleven of the twelve came from 'broken' homes.[5]

Race and ethnicity are just as important factors when looking at disaffection. In the UK, disproportionate numbers of African Caribbean children are doing badly in GCSEs: among those failing to get a single GCSE in 1996 were 9% of black pupils, 6% of white pupils, 5% of Asians (Indian, Pakistani, Bangladeshi) and 4% among other ethnic groups.[6] This is despite African Caribbean children slightly outperforming their white peers in reading and language tests.[7] Black children are also between four and six times more likely to be excluded than their white peers.

But despite these trends, more black and Asian young people than whites stay in full-time education in the UK, usually at colleges of further education. It is only young Bangladeshis who are the exception, neither attending post 16 education nor receiving training.[8] The minority group most at risk of failing and dropping out are Gypsy and Traveller children although they, like African Caribbeans, start off their schooling on a positive note. As with all children generally, but particularly for ethnic minorities, the transition to secondary school seems to be a flashpoint in their academic careers, with a crisis peak often at Year 9.

Gender is another significant indicator for school disaffection and underachievement. Chris Woodhead, Chief Inspector of Schools, has said that 'the failure of boys and in particular white working class boys is one of the most disturbing problems we face within the whole education system.'[9] In the United States, 'special education' classes for underachieving and disruptive students are largely black, Hispanic and 85% male.[10] In this country, 2,000 more boys than girls leave school without a single GCSE. At the top end of the ability scale, 50% of all girls receive five A-C grade GCSEs or GNVQ equivalents as opposed to 40% of boys.[11] But the gender divide isn't across the board. At the bottom end of achievement, the gap narrows, with 15% of girls leaving school without GCSEs compared with 19% of boys. Apart from a big discrepancy in English grades, the balance between low achieving boys and girls is about equal.[12]

Boys' underachievement in school is not a new phenomenon but our concern with it is, driven in part by the social and economic changes that have taken place in the last few decades. As David Jackson points out, 'In many boys' lives at school, there is a dynamic interaction between their social/economic worlds of failure, dependency and powerlessness and their deep investments in dominant forms of heterosexual masculinities... As a result, not working hard at school can be seen as a defensive strategy by some boys to distance themselves from an academic world that is perceived as dangerously 'weak.'[13]

Young people living in local authority care are one of the highest risk groups for low achievement, dropping out and exclusion. Over a quarter of 14 to 16 year olds in care are either persistent truants or have been excluded from school; and anywhere between half and three quarters of care leavers have no educational qualifications. The reasons are complex, ranging from the fundamental problems that have resulted in their being taken into care in the first place to being moved around frequently from one placement to another. These factors are often compounded by low expectations and low priority being placed on their education by carers and schools.[14]

The stakes are equally high for teenage mothers, although it's difficult to disentangle cause and effect. What is known is that early sexual activity is associated particularly with low socio-economic status and being in care. Almost 100,000 babies are born to teenage mothers in Britain every year – the highest rate in the European Union – including 9,000 to girls under the age of 16. Both teenage mothers and fathers come mainly from social classes III and IV; about one fifth of young women leaving care are either pregnant or are already mothers. According to the National Children's Bureau, 'Teenage mothers are less academically able than their childless contemporaries and more likely to leave school at the earliest opportunity with few or no qualifications.'[15]

Gay and lesbian youth are also at risk of dropping out because of the widespread homophobia that exists among staff and fellow pupils. In the United States the situation was highlighted by a 1996 watershed federal court judgment awarding Jamie Nabozny nearly one million dollars in a case against school administrators who failed to give protection to him during a period of time in which he suffered repeated verbal and physical attacks at school. A number of studies have revealed the prevalence of anti-gay attitudes in American schools. The most startling are those showing that 80% of prospective teachers admit to holding negative attitudes towards gay and lesbian people and the same percentage of gay and lesbian youth feeling severe social isolation.[16]

These statistics illuminate the broad sweep of social factors that contribute to children not fitting into school. Some fit into the stereotypes we have of the failing/truanting/disruptive student. But there are other stories the disaffected have to tell, too. An American study of eighth to tenth grade (14 to 16 year old) dropouts that looks at their reasons for leaving school show that over half said they couldn't get along with teachers. That old chestnut, the personality clash, is alive and well in schools, continues to make pupils' – and teachers' – lives a misery and may even be on the increase with larger class sizes and growing academic pressures.[17]

The disaffected can also be children who live with the daily threat of abuse in their own homes. Perhaps they have to care for a parent, grandparent or siblings. There are those who get no support from their parents or are being raised in hard-pressed single parent families. Some are undernourished and inadequately housed. Others are browbeaten and terrorised by violent gangs or bullies in a neighbourhood dominated by criminal sub-cultures. There are those who have been traumatised by having to leave their country under duress. And there are still others whose culture and language are different to those of the school or who experience discrimination and abuse because of their colour, cultural background, sexual orientation or religion.

There will be those, too, who don't fit into these categories. They may be middle class or from stable homes where emotional stress, perhaps as a result of family discord, has taken its toll on motivation, self-image and the ability to concentrate. They may be experiencing a bereavement or perhaps feelings of alienation that can overwhelm less resilient young people of all backgrounds in adolesence.

The whole area of special needs and behaviour is another factor in the picture of disaffection. When are children perceived as having emotional and behaviour difficulties (EBD) and when are they just girls and boys behaving badly? And what is the difference between each of these and disaffection? (See Chapter 3) We need to clarify these issues, along with the questions of how transient disaffection is and to what extent children's emotional and behaviour difficulties mask other problems such as dyslexia, Attention Deficit/Hyperactivity Disorder or milder forms of autism. We need to understand how and when the inability of a child to access the curriculum because of cognitive or emotional needs being unmet explodes into disruptive behaviour – or implodes into profound withdrawal and disengagement.

The inability of pupils to progress academically is yet another important consideration. Sometimes the failure to achieve will be due to un-detected cognitive disabilities, other times to a myriad of socio-economic factors that may not be addressed at primary level. An LEA giving evidence to the Commons' Education and Employment report on disaffection said: 'There is no doubt that the key [to disaffection] is to be found... in the early attainment of basic skills of literacy and numeracy, without which any secondary curriculum is unlikely to be truly available.' Other submissions from the Royal College of Paediatrics and Child Health pointed to chronic physical and mental health problems as being possible contributing factors.[18]

There is still much that needs to be understood about the correlation between special needs and disaffection. In the words of a senior civil servant at the Department for Education, 'It's one of the great imponderables.' What we do know is that pupils with special needs are eight times more likely to be excluded than those without statements. In addition, a 'significant' number of pupils who are at various stages of the special needs assessment process are being excluded. Those children with emotional and behaviour difficulties, with or without statements, are at particular risk of exclusion. Of special concern is the rise in the numbers of exclusions from EBD schools, although it is true that effective EBD schools exhaust all possible options before excluding a student.[19]

Looking at the big picture, the disaffected child is one who cannot or will not fit into the normal school structure and environment for a range of reasons that schools may or may not be aware of. Better communication between schools and home is an important element of education reform that leads to better understanding of the child's problems. It's an ideal that's not always easy to achieve, but must be worked at. Similarly and most fundamentally, schools must strive to offer an environment in which the diversity of needs that the young and disaffected bring with them is provided for. For that to happen, they need to have the mechanisms in place to identify those needs and the will and energy to change attitudes and structures.

References

1. Kinder, K., *et al* (1995) *Three to Remember*, National Foundation for Educational Research.

2. *Times Educational Supplement*, April 2 1999.

3. Radwanski, G. *Ontario study of the relevance of education and the issue of dropouts*, Ministry of Education, Ontario, 1987.

4. *Dreams Deferred: High school dropouts in the United States*, US Educational Testing Service, Princeton, New Jersey, 1995.

5. Smale, W. and da Costa, J. *Understanding the Issue of Dropouts: A Young Offender Perspective*, University of Alberta, Canada, 1999.

6. *Monitoring Poverty and Social Exclusion*, Joseph Rowntree Foundation, 1999.

7. Wright, C., Race *Relations in the Primary School*, David Fulton, 1992.

8. Pearce, N. and Hillman, J. *Wasted Youth*, IPPR, 1998.

9. *Times Educational Supplement*, March 15 1996.

10. Phillips, A. *The Trouble with Boys*, Pandora, 1993.

11. *Monitoring Poverty and Social Exclusion, op.cit.*

12. *Wasted Youth, op.cit.*

13. Jackson, D. 'Breaking out of the binary trap: boys' underachievement, schooling and gender relations' in *Failing Boys? Issues in Gender and Achievement* edited by Epstein, D. *et al*, Open University Press, 1999.

14. *The Education of Children who are Looked After by Local Authorities*, Department of Health/Ofsted, 1995.

15. *Times Educational Supplement*, March 19, 1999.

16. Duttweiler, P. (1997) 'Gay and Lesbian Youth at Risk,' *The Journal of At Risk Issues*, Volume 3, Winter/Spring.

17. *National Education Longitudinal Study of 1988-First Follow-up Study 1990*, U.S. Department of Education, National Centre for Education Statistics.

18. *Disaffected Children*, House of Commons Education and Employment Committee Fifth Report, Volume 1, The Stationery Office, April 1988.

19. *Social Inclusion: Pupil Support*. Draft Guidance, Department for Education and Employment, January 1999.

CHAPTER TWO
DROP-OUTS AND PUSHED-OUTS

Gee, Officer Krupke, we're very upset,
We never had the love that ev'ry child oughta get,
We ain't no delinquents, we're misunderstood,
Deep down inside us there is good.
There is good, there is untapped good,
Like inside, the worst of us is good!
('Officer Krupke,' lyrics by Steven Sondheim from
'West Side Story'*)

The young and disaffected take one of four routes in the education system. Either they are pushed out – excluded – or they truant persistently, fail their exams or drop out before taking them. Whatever direction they go in, they face a precarious future dogged by stigma, no qualifications and low self-esteem – with the attendant mental health problems that social exclusion brings.

Exclusions

Exclusion from school means being on the outside, alienated from the mainstream, feeling different from the norm, being unwanted by an institution that wants everybody else. It means being branded as a problem and carrying that problematic identity around with you, possibly for the rest of your life.

It means being placed in a special Pupil Referral Unit that may be able to get you on track but is more likely to reinforce your belief that you're ineducable and not cut out for 'normal' society. While there are some extremely good units (see Chapter 8 'The Search for Solutions'), the majority have been found by Ofsted to be institutions in which 'children are poorly served'. The alternative to a PRU is getting a few hours a week of home tuition. Young people may have to wait months for their 'education otherwise' to materialise and when it happens, they find that those few hours are a drop in the bucket when there are all those other hours – empty time with no structure, no supervision – to fill. Time to sleep, watch daytime telly, listen to music, get depressed, experiment with drugs, be out on the streets meeting other people with time on their hands...

Around half of all children permanently excluded are between Years 9 and 11, with boys outnumbering girls by 4:1 at secondary level and 12:1 at primary.[1]

While the government has committed itself to social inclusion, school exclusion rates have never been higher, having risen inexorably throughout the 1990s. To help meet its target of reducing exclusions by a third by the year 2002, it's come up with the idea of the pastoral support plan. This would keep disruptive students in class for up to four months before excluding them and the plan is to be designed to improve behaviour. In reality, it's yet another attempt to coerce schools into holding onto pupils who they'd rather be shot of. Given the track record of similar behaviour management schemes based on contracts between pupil and teacher that have cropped up in the past decade in response to exclusion rates having spiralled out of control, the proof of PSPs' effectiveness will have to be evaluated carefully to show that it's workable. What is certain is that contracts alone will not shift pupils' negative attitudes towards school; nor will it shift teachers' attitudes towards and expectations of pupils who are identified as being disruptive.

What is also clear is that desperate attempts to meet targets on reducing exclusion rates ignore the most pressing question facing educationalists in the whole debate about inclusion and disaffection, which is this: Are there some disaffected young people who, because of the nature and degree of their disruptive behaviour, can't and shouldn't be in mainstream? Despite the closing down of special schools, despite the move away from statementing by many LEAs, despite the impassioned crusade for inclusion by parents and educationalists that has been so influential in guiding public policy in recent years, is it in any child's or school's best interests to keep the most disruptive children in mainstream when the havoc they create around them makes it obvious that this is not where they belong? Is the sleight of hand being exercised by some 'fully inclusionist' LEAs in shunting their disaffected and/or EBD kids into neighbouring education authority's special schools fair to local families?

In the final analysis, we know that the practice of school exclusion is being abused in some cases. But if we as a society are as serious about social inclusion in all its manifest forms as government and school policies would indicate, we have to ask the uncomfortable question of whether the practice of inclusion is not being abused, too.

The reasons for the escalating exclusion rate (which, while going down for white children, continues to rise for black pupils) are various, but keys lie in the rise of poverty, the widening gap between rich and poor and the profound changes in the approach to schooling ushered in with the Education Reform Act 1988 and subsequent legislation.

Poverty and class

The impact of poverty on educational outcome and school attendance has been well-documented over the decades since the war. The latest report to examine the links comes from the Joseph Rowntree Foundation. Of a group of low income children involved in a longitudinal study carried out for the Foundation's project on Child Development and Family Income[2], 10% had school attendance below 0.75 at the age of 15. At the age of 23, 61% of the males who had had low school attendance still had no educational qualifications. Neither had the 48% who had been in trouble with the police during adolescence. A H Halsey summed it up when he wrote that despite working class students having gained increased access to some form of higher education over the years, ... 'class inequalities, measured in relative terms, have apparently remained stable for the past three generations'.[3]

The facade of choice and the realities of selection

The various education reforms over the past eleven years have also taken their toll on children at risk. The educational marketplace with its notion of parental choice has been exposed as bankrupt. What we have seen is choice remaining a prerogative of the educated and well-off who are in the right catchment areas for the good comprehensives, or who can pay for their children to be tutored for entrance exams to grammar or private schools. The rest have to settle for what they can get; and often that turns out to be struggling local comps which they and their children perceive as second best.

The unstoppable ascendancy of the grammar school is the cornerstone of inequity and inequality in the state system. In their selective corridors, poor children are notable for their absence. A recent study shows that in Liverpool for example, where 40% of secondary pupils receive free school dinners, only 6% of pupils at the Blue Coat selective school fall into that category. In other schools, it's fewer than that.

Although few in number, where they exist, grammar schools are responsible for creaming off the top (predominately middle class) pupils and leaving the local comprehensives as the domain of white and black working class pupils, and those with special needs children and children for whom English is an additional language. The social and ethnic apartheid of some areas on the basis of school is stark. Scottish studies on parental choice and open enrolment show that 'choice, operating largely, though not entirely, along social class lines, has the effect of reinforcing already existing social and educational divisions'.[4] By giving local parents the vote on whether to abolish or keep grammar schools, the government is cleverly extricating itself from a no-win situation. As I write this, the vote is imminent. Caroline St John-Brooks, editor of the *Times Educational Supplement* warns that opponents of grammar schools shouldn't count their chickens before they're hatched. 'The educational caste system,' she writes in a leader, 'is remarkably resilient'.[5]

How does this impact on disaffection? In a situation where the high achievers in a community are whisked away to separate schools – or are sent to beacon schools for fast-tracking in certain subjects – it sets up a domino effect of deficits in the local comprehensives that can spell disaster for all children but particularly for those whose connection with school is tenuous. When comprehensives contain less of a variation of abilities and class backgrounds, standards as measured in test results fall in reflection of the homogeneity of the pupil population. When test results are low, children perceive their schools as second best. When the collective self-esteem within a school is battered, behaviour and attendance suffer. When children act out and truant, teachers feel demoralised and stressed. When teachers are at a low ebb, teaching becomes lacklustre, attitudes towards pupils become punitive, everybody goes home unhappy – and some never come back.

The curriculum

The curriculum, too, has something to answer. The great watershed of latterday education reform, the national curriculum, has irrefutably resulted in improvements in general academic performance. But there has been a high price to pay. With a tightly packed and standardised academic curriculum predicated on reaching specific targets at each key stage has come the sidelining of creative expression, particularly in the arts, an area in which many less academic children are able to experience success and pleasure. The packed curriculum has also elbowed out the underpinnings of multiculturalism and antiracism, leaving ethnic minority children feeling marginalised and disengaged. In addition, positive affirmation of all children has been superceded by setting, which has been ushered in with great enthusiasm after having languished in the educational wilderness for some time. American studies have shown setting and other group differentiation to be a contributing factor to disaffection by negatively impacting on the self-esteem and motivation of children in the lower sets.

Lowering the profile

There is also evidence that schools are concentrating their energies more on the abler students to the detriment of bilingual children and ethnic minorities, white working class children and those with special needs.[6] Under-resourcing, with the introduction of Local Management of Schools, is partly to blame. But so too is the mentality that has surrounded the publication of league tables. The possibility of SATs and GCSE results being compromised by children with problems, whether they keep those problems to themselves or act out and cause disruption, is too great a risk for many schools to entertain. A zero tolerance approach to the disruptive or truanting pupil has developed in many schools with the full support of governors, leading them to exclude where once they would have brought in extra support.

Inadequate training

Finally, the changing nature of teacher training has contributed to a situation where many teachers feel ill-equipped to deal with children who don't conform to the norm. With the emphasis on curriculum and the bulk of training spent in practice, the theoretical framework that's needed to understand and deal with emotional and behaviour issues arising in the classroom, let alone straightforward child development, has been largely dropped. Faced with 26 or 30 pupils and a scheme of work that leaves little space in which to maneouvre, the teacher of to-day doesn't have the time, inclination or know-how to deal with the square pegs of this world. S/he's too busy pushing everyone else through the round holes.

Exclusions

Despite the government's commitment to cut exclusions by one third by the year 2002 and despite the introduction of strategies such as pastoral support plans to keep disruptive children in schools, the numbers paint a picture of schools no longer able – or willing – to cope with difficult behaviour. In 1990/91, 2,910 children were excluded from English schools; by 1996/97 (latest figures available from the Department for Education and Employment) the number had skyrocketed to 12,700. An independent survey of local education authorities conducted by Carl Parsons of Canterbury Christ Church College put those figures somewhat higher, at 13,453. Primary school exclusions accounted for 1,600; special schools excluded 600 in 1996/7, an increase of 21% from the previous year. All told, this represents a six-fold rise in seven years.

Race and ethnicity

Ethnicity is a major issue in this sorry picture. The ethnic breakdown of exclusions shows a disproportionate number of African Caribbean boys being excluded: they are between four and six times more likely to be thrown out of school than their white counterparts. Where the exclusion rate for white pupils is 0.18%, for African Caribbeans it is 0.76%. As David Gillborn, lecturer in sociology at the London Institute of Education puts it, 'The Department for Education's own statistics suggest that exclusions are operating in a racialised fashion, such that

African Caribbean students are disproportionately denied even basic access to education institutions – let alone substantive access to educational opportunities within schools'.[7]

What researchers tells us is that there are two major factors that contribute to this trend. One is racial tension, often taking the form of bullying or name-calling in the playground. When the black or ethnic minority child is provoked and fights back, they may be held responsible for the trouble, instead of the teacher or headteacher attempting to put the whole incident in context. The second phenomenon is the misinterpretation of black children's behaviour. There has been much documentation of classroom interactions to show that, in the words of Cecile Wright, 'teacher and pupil relationships are mediated by ethnicity.' She borrows the term coined by Figueroa, 'racial frame of reference,' to explain how teachers view and classify their pupils.[8] A typical perception is that African Caribbean children are troublemaking, loud and disruptive and that boys, particularly older ones, are aggressive. (See Chapter 4 'Race and Culture Clash').

We haven't even hit the tip of the iceberg in coming to grips with what the report of the Macpherson Commission's inquiry into the murder of Stephen Lawrence identified as the institutional racism that pervades our society, from the police force to the media to our schools. Even if Macpherson's recommendations that schools embrace antiracism and multiculturalism are to be implemented with the help of an amended National Curriculum – which looks unlikely – schools would need much more support to reverse the trends implicit in the exclusion figures.

The negative dynamics that lead to high black exclusion rates will only begin to be tackled when the attitudes and preconceptions of teachers *vis a vis* race and ethnicity are addressed. That process must start by re-examining how teacher training prepares teachers for racial and cultural diversity in the classroom. Mairtin Mac an Ghaill described the consequences of not doing so based on a study he undertook. 'There may be no conscious attempt to treat black youth in a different way to white youth, but the unintended teacher effects result in differential responses which work against black youth. African-Caribbean students tended to be seen as having 'low ability' and potential discipline problems'.[9]

Current teacher training allows classroom teachers to reinforce racial stereotypes and place the responsibility for a black child's unpopularity or underperformance on the child itself and not the teaching, as Russell Jones' research illustrates.[10]

Other disproportionately represented groups among students who are excluded are teenage mothers and young people in local authority care. Each are 80 times more likely to be excluded from school than children who live at home.

Exclusion is something of a life sentence. According to the National Exclusions Reporting System, two out of every three students who are permanently excluded fail to secure a place in a mainstream school. Whether they are sent to Pupil Referral Units or receive home tuition, the likely outcome is that they lose the plot as far as their education is concerned once they've been excluded. They become true outsiders – and all too often, being outside school leads to being outside the law. Of all the juvenile crime committed, over one-third takes place during school hours either by those who are truanting or have been excluded or by those who don't have a school place.[11]

Truancy

> *...how schools operate can make a great difference in shaping whether children...truant.* (Truancy and Social Exclusion Report, Social Exclusion Unit, 1998)

About a million children every year – 37% of boys and 28% of girls – skip school for at least a half a day. The average for primary school children is five days; for secondary, it's ten days a year.[12] Other figures suggest the problem is much greater. A DfEE study of nearly 38,000 students surveyed for the Truancy Unit found nearly one third claiming they had truanted at least once during the past six weeks; among the 16 year olds, 10% said they bunked off at least once a week.[13]

The government's response has been to declare a commitment to reducing truancy by one third by the year 2002 and to set up a number of special projects, the latest of them New Start, to address attendance, behaviour and underachievement.

While the archetypal truant is male and up to no good, the true picture is far more complex and variable. The reasons for not going to school range from wanting to avoid specific lessons, teachers or tests, to the fear of being bullied, to having to look after siblings at parents' demand. Others claim that parents know about their truanting even if they are not directly responsible for their absence. Many say that school is boring or irrelevant.

Whatever the reasons for bunking off, truants fall into two distinct categories: the blanket truant who stays away from school altogether and the post-registration truant, who hangs around for registration in the morning and then scarpers for some or all of the lessons.[14] D.J. O'Keeffe, the author of two reports on truancy in English schools, found in 1994 that 66% of secondary school pupils, mostly in years 10 and 11, said they bunked off, half of them admitting to doing so post registration to avoid particular lessons that they didn't like.[15]

A report by the Institute for Public Policy Research highlights the fact that truancy among girls has been overshadowed by the more disruptive symptoms of male disaffection. Girls are more likely to act out their disengagement with school and problems in their lives not through bad behaviour or even necessarily persistent truanting, but by missing occasional classes and underachieving.[16]

While truancy and dropping out are difficult to disentangle one from the other, we do know that there is a significant number of young people who give up on school altogether. Measuring this by percentages entering for GCSE exams, 14% of 16 year olds were either not entered for their exams or achieved no passes at all according to 1994 figures for England. In 1996, the figure was somewhere between 45,000 and 50,000.

The prognosis for these young people is not good. An extrapolation of figures by the Youth Cohort Survey suggest that dropouts who fit into the Status Zero category of being in neither education, training nor employment at age 16 were in the same position two years later.[17]

There in body but not in mind

Absence of occupation is not rest
A mind quite vacant is a mind distressed.
'Retirement' by William Cowper (1731-1800)

In 'Playing Truant in Mind: the social exclusion of quiet pupils'[18] Janet Collins argues that the focus on school attendance has obscured another serious manifestation of disaffection: the child who attends school but is disengaged, because of either inability or unwillingness to particpate in the act of learning. She borrows the term 'truant in mind' from Young[19] to describe the withdrawn, non-participatory behaviour that every teacher is familiar with. These are the pupils who will do the minimum of work and appear disinterested in what is going on in the classroom. It is a notoriously difficult problem to deal with. Perhaps most problematic is identifying it in the first place. All children – indeed all adults, too – go mentally off task from time to time. But true truancy in the mind is a habitual behaviour in which withdrawal con- sistently impacts negatively on work that the child produces.

Although there is no research to indicate how widespread a problem this is, Collins' own small scale longitudinal study of ten girls and two boys in a Year 6 class offers insights into this common yet easy to over- look form of dropping out. She found that children have different strategies for avoiding engagement in classroom activities, which she chacterises as being invisible, refusing to participate, hesitation and in- appropriate focus. Most worrying was the chicken and egg syndrome of disengagement: while the child would often recoil from participating because of shyness and/or low self-esteem, their withdrawal – and the common response of teachers to turn a blind eye to their withdrawal – further exacerbated the child's negative self-image. To make matters even worse, once children saw that withdrawal made them invisible to the teacher – or that their social awkwardness disinclined the teacher to interact with them – there was no reason for them to keep their mind on what was happening in the class: they knew that the teacher wouldn't call on them. And so they could sit there in their shells, day in, day out, a physical presence but mentally and spiritually absent.

The costs of social exclusion

Whichever way you look at it, the costs of disaffection are high. On the human scale, the failure that is often the end of the road for excluded, disruptive and truanting students can mean the end of the road for aspirations to a decent job, home and lifestyle too. In terms of academic achievement, there's a simple corollary between being in school and learning and not being in school and failing. Truants miss out to a devastating degree. Nearly 38% of truants leave school without a single GCSE, compared with three per cent of regular attenders; and only eight per cent of truants achieve five or more grade A to C GCSEs, compared to over half of those who go to school regularly.[20]

Girls who become alienated from school run an increased risk of getting pregnant. Britain holds the worst records in western Europe for teenage pregnancies, at 33 births for every thousand girls aged between 15 and 19: five times the rate of Holland. In 1996, the number of girls conceiving before age 16 was the highest ever recorded, at 4,279.[21]

Drifting into crime is a major risk for boys who lose the plot at school. In fact, the highest risk factor for youth crime is absence from school. Almost 95% of boys in young offender institutions have either been excluded from school, persistently truanted or dropped out before reaching their 16th birthday, according to a survey by the National Association for the Care and Resettlement of Offenders. As well as their lives being wasted, taxpayers' pounds are, too. Every young offender costs at least £75,000 a year to keep in prison.[22] A total of £70 million of public money is spent in the courts, young offenders insitutions and the probation service. While two thirds of young offenders have effectively dropped out of society and exist at status zero, where they are neither in education, training or work, there is little evidence of social workers and probation officers addressing their education problems.[23]

In all, there are between 100,000 and 220,000 young people between the ages of 14 and 19 – children leaving care, the homeless, young offenders, teenage mothers, drug users as well as those who don't fit into those categories but have dropped out of school or been excluded – who fall into the netherworld of status zero. They are dispossessed, directionless young people who are neither in education, employment nor training, whose horizons don't stretch beyond tomorrow and who, whether they know it or not, have everything to fear for the future. These young people, who move in and out of the margins of society, constitute 16% of their peer group: 7 to 8% of 16 year olds and 8 to 9% of 17 year olds. While their fate can't be solely laid at the door of schools, the failure of the education system to connect with them on some level is an undeniable factor in their inability to see their schooling through. The government's aim to reduce the number of young people leaving school without any GCSEs has, by definition, to take into account the fact that school isn't relevant to these kids lurking in the shadows.

Clearly, if the tide is to turn so too must policies, attitudes, structures. The system must be more responsive to the various needs, backgrounds and abilities of all students while not compromising standards and expectations for the more able end of the spectrum. The response must be structural and comprehensive in scope. A tall order? You bet. Impossible? Take a look at the American models documented in Chapter 4. When the will is there, the right thinking and available resources can be found.

References

1. Parsons, C. *Demonising, Pathologising and Educational Exclusion: The English Response to 'Behaviour Problems'*, BERA 1998.
2. Joseph Rowntree Foundation, 1999.
3. 'Trends in access and equity in higher education', *Oxford Review of Education*, 19 (2), 1993.
4. Smith, T. *et al.*, *Education Divides: Poverty and Schooling in the 1990s*, Child Poverty Action Group, 1995.
5. St John Brooks, C. (May 28 1999) 'Equality 2000?', *Times Educational Supplement*.
6. *Times Educational Supplement*, April 2 1999.
7. Gillborn, D. *Racism and Antiracism in Real Schools*, Open University Press, 1985.
8. Wright, C. *Race Relations in the Primary School*, David Fulton, 1992.
9. Mac an Ghaill, M. *Young, Gifted and Black: Student-Teacher Relations in the Schooling of Black Youth*, Open University Press, 1988.
10. Jones, Russell, *Teaching Racism – or Tackling It? Multicultural Stories from White Beginning Teachers*, Trentham 1999
11. *Monitoring Poverty and Social Exclusion*, ibid.
12. *Truancy and Social Exclusion Report*, Social Exclusion Unit, 1998.
13. O'Keeffe, D.G. *Truancy in English Secondary Schools*, HMSO, 1994.

14. O'Keeffe, D.G. (1981) 'Labour in Vain: Industry, Truancy and the Social Curriculum'. In Flew, A. (ed.) 'The Pied Pipers of Education', Social Affairs Unit.

15. O'Keeffe, D.G. *Truancy in English Schools*, ibid.

16. *Wasted Youth*, IPPR, 1998.

17. *Disaffected Children* Volume 1, House of Commons Education and Employment Committee, The Stationery Office, April 1998

18. BERA, 1998.

19. Young, D. *Knowing How and Knowing That*, Birkbeck College, 1984.

20. *Truancy and Social Exclusion Report*, Social Exclusion Unit, 1999.

21. *Monitoring Poverty and Social Exclusion*, ibid.

22. *Wasted Lives*, NACRO, 1998.

23. Audit Commmission, 1998.

CHAPTER THREE

HOW MAINSTREAM WORKS AGAINST THE DIFFERENT CHILD

A culture which leaves unsatisfied and drives to rebelliousness so large a number of its members neither has a prospect of continued existence nor deserves it. (Sigmund Freud, 'The Future of an Illusion').

We face a dilemma in education as we enter the new millennium: do we adhere to the basic structures and content that have defined our schools for the past 120 years, a status quo which has adequately served the majority but not the minority? Or do we take the plunge and look for new, unconventional approaches that embrace those who don't fit as well into school?

In Britain, some answers to the dilemma have already been found. As we've seen, the growing popularity of the grammar school over the past decade has created a rather dubious third way. Though few in number, they have made an enormous impact in the areas where they are found, leaving the less able and less affluent as the major users of the local comprehensives. While there are still good neighbourhood schools with reasonable social and ethnic mixes, they are becoming more and more over-subscribed, creating situations where waiting lists are growing longer and longer and parents who are denied access because of reduced catchment areas are growing ever more desperate. Because of the lack of suitable alternatives, those with the resources are compelled to move to areas with better schools. If they can't afford to, they consign their children to their fate in the local school and hope for the best.

The notion of parental choice has transformed the way the 'consumer' looks at schools and the way we measure their success. The unstoppable rise of the grammar school is just one example of this. Even more fundamentally, it has defined how schools prioritise the services they provide. A broad-based, inclusive curriculum that aims to produce well-rounded, socially and emotionally developed individuals is not what education in 1990s Britain was about. Looking strong in the league tables was. Invariably, the top schools have been selective and have ploughed their considerable energies and resources into ensuring that children get the highest marks possible. School ethos in these schools is dominated by high achievement; support for the laggers, the strugglers, the kids who are losing the plot because of the pressures being put on them is, in many of these schools, paltry if not non-existent. At an open evening for prospective parents at a phenomenally popular grammar school in north London a few years ago, a parent asked the headteacher what support there was for children with special needs. 'We have no special needs here,' retorted the head unapologetically. That is the bottom line of the grammar schools on which the middle classes have built their hopes and aspirations.

With the gathering political and economic momentum for inclusive education, the grammar schools – if local parents vote to keep them – will enjoy the status of being ever more clamoured-for sanctuaries of good behaviour and high achievement while the comprehensives struggle further under unprecedented pressures to absorb children with a wide range of special needs, many of whom would formerly not have been mainstreamed. To help them deal with pupils with challenging behaviour, the government has announced an injection of half a billion pounds to bring into operation a range of mechanisms to fight truancy and exclusion. It is a bold step. It will need to be, to foot the substantial bills and to find the expertise needed to train teachers and equip schools to face the new challenges ahead.

Certainly some of the very interesting proposals included in the government's draft guidance on 'Social Inclusion: Pupil Support,'[1] are already proving controversial. The Pastoral Support Programme, for instance, which compels schools to wait 16 weeks before excluding a disruptive child, is a bid to deal with the vertiginous exclusion rates in a way that, some fear, is unworkable. The impact that this period of grace could have on other children in the classroom, as well as on teachers, is liable to be great. Professionals working in the EBD field know that there are some children who need to be separate, for their own sake as well as for the sake of everybody else.

There are other approaches in the document which also look good but beg questions of realistic implementation. For instance, in dealing with signs of disaffection, there is an emphasis on parents coming to talk to teachers about concerns they have about their child's attitude to school as part of the home-school agreement. Parents have responsibility in ensuring that their children come to school on time, stay in school and abide by behaviour policies and other school rules. They are assumed to know how their child is doing at school and if and when there are problems. But in reality, disaffection at school may not be transferred to home in a way that parents can easily interpret. Or, as is often the case, it may be that a child is using school to act out difficulties that are occurring at home where there is an environment that is unsupportive and unresponsive to their needs – or worse. Or it may be that the disaffected school pupil is uncommunicative at home or puts on a veneer of everything being okay to avoid parents' concern. Or, lastly, it may be that the troubled child is in care and there is simply no one with whom schools can liaise on this sort of level.

An EBD child by any other name?

The discussion around inclusion has thrown up other issues, too. One is that the distinction between disaffection and EBD has been blurred beyond recognition. As Professor Harry Daniels of Birmingham University's EBD Team puts it:

> The term disaffection is fraught with difficulties. We're seeing it being used more and more interchangeably with the term EBD. The fact is that they're not the same. It's possible to have a child with EBD who isn't disaffected. More generally, there are significant concerns that children's emotional needs are not being understood and responded to in schools.

Is the distinction important? It is for those concerned with providing the appropriate support. As the Department for Education and Employment states:

> Emotional and behavioural difficulties lie on the continuum between behaviour which challenges teachers but is within normal,

albeit unacceptable bounds and that which is indicative of serious mental illness...The distinction between normal but stressed behaviour, emotional and behavioural difficulties and behaviour arising from mental illness is important because each needs to be treated differently.[2]

But who makes those distinctions in an education system where children rarely see educational psychologists – let alone get statements of special needs – and where teachers are often too preoccupied with the pressing demands of full classrooms and crammed curricula to focus on the child whose behaviour is out of the ordinary? Maureen Smith, deputy headteacher of New Rush Hall School for children with emotional and behavioural difficulties in the London Borough of Redbridge, offers her perceptions on the difference between the two categories:

> Children with EBD experience their difficulties everywhere they go: at school, at Sainsbury's, at the park. They're not able to contain their emotions. It's not within their cognitive reach. Disaffected children, on the other hand, have the ability to chose how to behave in different contexts. Their problem – their disaffection – is more specifically focused on school. The children we work with aren't necessarily disaffected. But some of them will wind up killing someone. They're the most disturbed kids around.

While children with emotional and behaviour difficulties have a complex set of problems which may go on for a number of years and often require specialist expertise, disaffected children may be going through a temporary bad time due to circumstances such as bereavement, bullying, or change of family circumstances. Or they may, because of the sometimes nihilistic ravages of adolescence, decide that school has no meaning for them. They may display emotional and behavioural difficulties, but the degree will vary from one child to another. The pre-eminent shared experience of disaffected pupils is that they have difficulties with school, whether it's with the learning itself or with the structures or social aspects; whether their problems are manifested as withdrawal or as truancy or as disruptive behaviour. Terry Emerson, who has worked in pupil referral units for many years, points to the ambiguities of the term when he says: 'Disaffection is a word used to describe any child or youth who doesn't fit into any other category and who nobody knows what to do with.'

John D'Abbro, headteacher of New Rush Hall School for EBD Children in the London Borough of Redbridge, agrees that disaffection and emotional and behaviour difficulties have become catch-alls for describing children who don't fit into the norm:

> Some youngsters we get here are inappropriately referred; we find that some schools under-refer while others over-refer. It comes down to the tolerance levels and expectations of management. Most teachers will tell you that the one thing that causes the most stress is disruptive behaviour. And that is escalating with the increasing numbers of pupils going to school and feeling disenfranchised by the system because they're not getting grades – because they have trouble with the curriculum and aren't getting the help they need – and then being told that there's no paid employment for people who don't get grades.

Disruptive behaviour may also be exacerbated by the inability of teachers to cope with increasing numbers of children acting out an ever-growing number of problems in their classrooms. As one Key Stage 2 teacher put it, 'A lot of disruption is the teachers' fault – we pitch the lesson wrong. This happens because we often focus on the demands of the curriculum and cannot devote so much attention to the needs of the children.' Another teacher from a behaviour support team, concurs:

> I've come across situations of youngsters getting into trouble in some classes that needn't have happened at all. It's a blunder that the teacher's made with that youngster. I've seen youngsters needlessly wound up to the point of conflict by being handled badly: it's a staff training issue.[3]

Chalkface issues

With the widening gap between rich and poor, the increase in divorce rates and the closure of special schools, the children pouring into schools every day of the week are bringing with them heavy baggage indeed. How teachers are expected to deal with the volume and diversity of problems they are presented with is a hotly debated issue. It is something the government is producing whole forest-loads of papers about and which the embryonic Education Action Zones are ostensibly attempting to address.

But the fact is that all the strategies, policies, draft guidances and proposals for new programmes that are coming in thick and fast have omitted to confront head-on the nuts and bolts chalkface issues surrounding teachers' attitudes and expertise. With the overwhelming emphasis of teacher training and in-service training on the curriculum, teachers are simply not getting the theoretical and practical frameworks they need to equip them to handle students who are difficult or uncommunicative. And so schools' tolerance levels become lower and lower and exclusions – often a succession of fixed term suspensions which may or may not lead to permanment exclusion – become more frequent.

Teachers' tolerance levels are the stock in trade of Australian behaviour management guru Bill Rodgers, who travels the world training teachers in how to manage the wide range of behaviours they face everyday. Part of his approach is helping teachers to respond appropriately to difficult situations, whether they're presented by children identified as EBD, the disaffected or just plain wind-ups.

He is particularly concerned about teachers who practice what he calls 'manic vigilance', that hyped-up state of red alert well-known to teachers who always expect trouble. These are the type of teachers who jump on every infraction and interruption, however small, while ignoring the primary, underlying problems. While this obviously doesn't apply to serious disruptions requiring equally serious interventions, Rodgers has suggestions for the common or garden variety of challenges that crop up many times a day. To summarise his approach: he recommends that teachers take a position of 'relaxed vigilance': keep the voice calm but firm, make behavioural directions as brief and positive as you can, give the impression of being in control and give students a choice of options on how they will proceed. 'The key is avoiding unnecessary confrontation and never embarrassing the child.'

While this may be easier said than done in a classroom of 25 plus children, a proportion of whom would rather be somewhere else, it's eminently realistic when you have a smaller group to deal with, no matter how disaffected they are.

Pupil referral units: the bad news and the good news

Pupil referral units have all the makings of being places where teachers have the leeway to work supportively and constructively with students who have dropped out or have been excluded from school because of difficult behaviour or repeated truancy. Size is on the side of PRUs. They are small and there are generally high staff to student ratios. Unfortunately, many have been found to be nothing more than sin bins by another name, holding stations that, in the view of an Ofsted report, 'lacked a clear purpose and challenge.'4 A 1995 inspection of the units found generally that 'intellectual stimulus was weak and the work was well below pupils' age and ability' although behaviour and attendance of pupils was improved. In fifteen of the twenty three units inspected, 'standards of work had major deficiencies and were often poor... [stemming] from a lack of planning; objectives were unclear and tasks were poorly matched to their ability despite the differences in age and ability in some groups of pupils'. Inspectors found in these underperforming PRUs that low expectations bred low standards of achievement, attendance and behaviour. When, instead of working to motivate students, PRUs' curricular work is focused on worksheets and 'set exercises often shorn of context and relevance,' it's hardly surprising that pupils' educational horizons remain low. Although the units are meant to reintegrate pupils back into mainstream, fewer than 40% of permanently excluded pupils return to ordinary schools.

There are, thankfully, exceptions to this rule that tend to take a more holistic view towards their work, combining high expectations with strong personal and social support. It's necessary not only because of students' failure in mainstream, but also as a way of dealing with the devastating experience. Jane Wharton, who set up the Cave school, a small pupil referral unit for pupils under 16 years old in south London twenty two years ago, echoes John D'Abbro's disquiet about tolerance and the reasons for its variability. 'In this area, it's the white working class kids who truant and drop out while the African Caribbean kids are excluded. We have to acknowledge that part of education is about social control.'

Her students over the years have ranged from the illiterate to high achievers. One boy was referred because of depression. He now has a degree in geology. Those of her students who dropped out rather than being pushed out have done so for a range of reasons. Some are trivial. 'They might have been shouted at by a teacher at the age of twelve and never got it sorted out. Or it might be that parents see school as an institution run by the enemy.' When they come to the Cave, which is a tiny school staffed by 2.5 teachers for up to fourteen students, they want to be there and do well. 'These kids want to belong somewhere. They have no family life, there's no communication at home. Here, they do five or six GCSEs and quite a lot of them get A to Cs, with particularly good results in English, art and enviornmental studies.' Most importantly, they get intensive attention there and, because teachers have regular consultations with a child psychotherapist, as much psychological as academic support. 'I talk a lot with teachers about where education ends and social work or psychotherapy begins,' says Wharton. What the Cave manages to do, because of its size and its commitment to its pupils, is to see its function as a seamless synthesis of the two.

Another PRU that has broken the mould is New Rush Hall Senior Annexe, which was set up by the London Borough of Redbridge as an adjunct to John D'Abbro's EBD school down the road (which also has an outreach programme, working with at risk pupils in mainstream). Run for children in Years 10 and 11, some of whom have been excluded from the EBD school, it has been given full marks by Ofsted, which puts it in its top ten of PRUs in the country. Arranged on two sites, it offers straight academic instruction as well a vocational component where students can do GCSEs in digital photography – it's the only school in the country with custom-designed, state of the art facilities for this – as well as music engineering and art. Last year, out of 22 students, 20 received A stars in GCSE art. Headteacher Terry Emerson has arranged things so that his Year 11 students are getting essentially one on one or one on two tuition in their academic subjects, which is what enables these kids, some of whom have entered the unit functionally illiterate the year before, to pass their GCSEs. Ofsted has said of this arrangement:

> The generous level of resourcing contributes significantly to the good progress made by pupils both in terms of academic outcomes and their attitudes to learning. The quality of teaching and the support and guidance offered to pupils are good and the curriculum

provided is satisfactory. Pupils are motivated by both high levels of staff contact and by access to high quality resources.

There aren't many sin bins you could say that about.

It's interesting to note that out of the forty students presently enrolled, only eight have statements for EBD and moderate learning difficulties. But many more clearly have cognitive difficulties that have stood in the way of their learning. Most are on average more than four years behind expectations in their reading when they enter; 40% have reading ages of 5 to 7 year olds. Even so, by Year 11 they are all doing six or seven GCSEs and get results that, given where they were the year before, are quite good. Out of twenty students, sixteen gained a pass in English and twelve in maths.

Pupils come to New Rush Hall Senior Annex because, in the words of headteacher Terry Emerson, 'no one else wants them.' Around 65% have had contact with the police. The week before I visited, ten police had surrounded the grotty pre-fab in which the unit is housed to arrest a 14 year old student. One of the officers said to Emerson, 'You don't have to go back into the classroom, Mr Emerson. He's dangerous.' 'I told him 'no he's not. I've been teaching him for six months'. Here was a boy who had committed seventeen previous offences, the latest one Actual Bodily Harm. But when he's here, he's a pussycat.' Last year, six of his students took their exams at Feltham Young Offenders Institution and the recidivism rate is 20%. But eight out of ten of the students go onto further education or employment.

Terry Emerson has been in charge of the PRU for six years, after working in a similar facility in Camden. It was in that education authority in the mid '80s that concern about disaffection in girls being overlooked led to a policy where 49% of PRU places were kept open for girls and training was given to teachers on the danger signs to look out for in girls:

> It took teachers in Camden three years of training and discussion to be able to recognise the signals that girls were giving. Truancy is a big factor for girls. When they're in school, a lot of teachers don't believe that they're acting out because they tend not to do it in front of the teachers. Instead, they play out their disaffection by

being withdrawn, by not interacting and not working. Because teachers only see problems when they flare up, girls who are truant in the mind are being ignored because the boys' over-acting-out gets all the attention.

He hasn't had the same success in Redbridge, where referrals of girls are very low. At present, they make up 20% of his PRU's intake; last year, it was only 2%. He has instituted a policy, however, that the unit won't accept less than five or six girls together at one time, in order to give them 'a fighting chance. Otherwise, it's not fair to them – we'd be setting them up to fail.' Or worse. In an overwhelmingly tough, male environment, a minority of girls in a unit could be especially vulnerable. As well as clearly not meeting the needs of all the quiet, withdrawn, disengaged girls who are invisibly letting go in mainstream, Emerson is all too aware of the impact that an absence of girls has on the boys in the unit. Even troubled, disruptive girls have a positive influence. 'They actually raise the achievement and behaviour of the boys. Because they have no girls to mix with, our boys have lower expectations.'

The particular pressures that many girls live with are an important piece of the disaffection jigsaw that schools aren't aware of, warns Emerson. Given the large numbers of children from single parent households who wind up in PRUs, there needs to be a greater awareness of the fact that single parents rely far more heavily on girls than boys for practical help. Where boys aren't generally given (or agree to carry out) jobs at home to help the hard-pressed single mother, girls are made to carry the load, doing everything from cooking and cleaning to shopping to looking after younger children. He believes that those added pressures work against girls' ability to engage with school. They also often lead them to become sexually active at a younger age than their peers as an act of emotional hunger. A report by Rathbone CI, a charity working with disaffected young people, has highlighted the second class treatment girls get in the provision of specialist services for emotional and behaviour difficulties because of the predominance of boys in this category. The charity, along with some smaller education authorities, has called for better planning to go into services for girls on a regional level, so that resources can be better coordinated and pooled.

The two 14 year old girls I spoke to on my visit to the PRU both had histories of violence at school and were articulate in recounting the reasons for it. Both had felt alienated and were convinced that they were victims of injustice at their previous schools by teachers and headteachers who 'had it out for them'. I've used pseudonyms.

Alesha is a softly and well-spoken African Caribbean girl, very attractive and high-achieving. She has four siblings (from two different fathers, neither of whom lives with the family) and her mother is pregnant with a fifth. She says her mother 'had the same problems as me when she went to school,' going to eight different schools because of disruptive behaviour. In spite of this, the mother did well at school and got into law school but had to drop out when she got pregnant. 'It was downhill for her from there.' Alesha has been excluded from two schools, both times for fighting.

At my first school, everything was going alright until in Year 8 a teacher asked me in class what profession I wanted to do and I said I wanted to be a paediatrician. From that moment, everything went against me. The other girls bullied me and the teacher was mean to me. Then one day, a girl hit me during break and I hit back and broke her nose. The next day her friends came at me with knives. I was sent to another school where there were only about twenty black students. There was a racist thing going on there. The first thing that happened was in one of my classes, a white girl shouted something rude to me and I said 'don't say that to me' and the teacher told me off and tried to get me out of the class. I said 'no' but I went in the end. My mum came into school and sorted things out but there were still problems with the teacher. Then another day two girls jumped me after school and called me racist names. I beat one of them and then there were phone calls from the girls saying 'we'll get you for racial assault, you black bitch.' My mum told the school about it and for the next five months I was made to sit in the office and do my work in there and eat my lunch in there. I was made to come into school late and leave early to avoid the other girls. I was the victim but the school made me feel like I was guilty.

After that, my mum took me out of the school. She went to the education department and said 'it's not working, you've sent her to the most racist school'. She asked for me to have home tuition. I was at home for seven and half months without any tuition. Finally, they referred me here. I was shocked and was afraid it would stay on my record and mess up my education that I was going to a PRU for bad kids. But it's the best thing that could've happened to me. At my last school, one of the teachers told my mum that with my attitude and my marks, the only future I had was working in a supermarket. Here, I'm getting all A's and everyone behaves well. I'm glad of what happened to me because it got me here. If I was still in mainstream, I'd be fighting.

The thing is, when you hold all your feelings inside of you, it causes trouble. I cried for three days the last time my mum laid into me and then I went and beat up my brother.

Charlene is a white working class girl, big and mature looking for her age, who has been in care for two years in three different placements, including a residential home. She has been with her current foster parents for ten months. Her parents are divorced and her mother, who has chronic mental health problems, is remarried. She has twin brothers and another sibling. Her behaviour with boys and male staff is highly sexualised.

My other school was a complete shit hole. I didn't get along with three teachers. I couldn't stand the fact that they looked down on you. I'm always told that I'm mature for my age and I can have a perfectly good conversation about Kosovo or whatever with adults. But these teachers would stand above you and say 'I'm big and you're small, you'll do what I say'. I've coped with being pushed around all my life. I can take my mother calling me a slut, slag and bitch. But I can't stand the attitude from teachers that I'm worthless and stupid.

I'd been expelled once for a few days when I got into a row with the deputy head because I was reading something and she told me to stop. I said 'up yours' and she excluded me. But the final crunch came when I freaked out at school a couple of months ago. I'd gone home to my mother's at lunchtime when I wasn't supposed to. She verbally abused me and when I got back to school I just lost it and threw things around. That's when I was kicked out of school. That was the only time anyone took notice of me at that school.

I was referred here and when I first came I thought this is the worst place you can be sent to. I saw it as another punishment. But I'm so glad I came. The thing about this school is that the teachers' honesty is amazing. If you're doing crap or you're acting like a dick-head, they'll tell you that you're acting stupid. They talk to you on your own level, not like you're down there and they're up here. I can honestly say that before I came here I didn't think I'd get any GCSEs. Now I know I can and I want to study to be a lawyer.'

Both girls wrap their stories up with happy endings. Unfortunately, it's not quite like that. Both still live lives that are the reason for their volatility and vulnerability. Alesha's mother is violent ('she says it's her pregnancy hormones') and while the girl appears to be on an even keel now, she could erupt the moment someone crosses her path. Charlene, despite her declared aspirations, speaks regularly of suicide, has harmed herelf and displays sexually provocative behaviour that could end in pregnancy sooner rather than later.

Terry Emerson is clear about the perameters of what he does. 'This place isn't the answer to any of their problems. All we can do is provide a structure for them.' While there is no formal counselling on site, he provides one on one counselling informally, on demand. A trained counsellor, he initially ran counselling sessions every morning but found that 'everybody clammed up.' Now, he finds that as he walks around the room, kids will let him know if they need to talk to him and he can withdraw them from the classroom. He also refers students to counsellors when necessary.

Looking at the way the Cave and New Rush Hall PRU work, it's hard not to be impressed. The buildings may be ugly, the windows may be barred, but the commitment that teachers give to these kids who no one else wants is inspiring. Well-resourced enough to provide teacher child ratios that ensure individualised attention, they work intensively not only to educate but to give their pupils something that no one else has given them: a sense of their worth and a belief in their ability to do something with their lives. Conveying that to a child who has been rejected by other teachers, other schools and sometimes their own parents goes beyond professionalism. It draws on teachers' humanity. And although all teachers in all schools, no matter how big or small, have it, there is something about working in a large institution that pushes it into the background far too often.

References

1. *Draft Guidance Social Inclusion: Pupil Support*, Department for Education and Employment, January 1999.

2. *The Education of Children with Emotional and Behavioural Difficulties*, Circular 9/94 DHLAC[94]9.

3. Kinder, K. *et al*, *Three to Remember: Strategies for Disaffected Pupils*, National Foundation for Educational Research, 1995.

4. *Pupil Referral Units – The first twelve inspections*, Office for Standards in Education, 1995.

CHAPTER FOUR
RACE AND CULTURE CLASH

It is a great shock at the age of five or six to find that in a world of Gary Coopers you are the Indian. James Baldwin in a 1965 speech to the Cambridge Union.

Education has a major role to play in countering racism which still persists in Britain today... A crucial element is to seek to identify and remove practices and procedures which work, directly or indirectly, and intentionally or unintentionally, against pupils from any ethnic group and to promote, through the curriculum, an appreciation and commitment to the principles of equality and justice, on the part of all pupils.

That excerpt from the 1985 Committee of Inquiry into the Education of Children from Ethnic Minority Groups, otherwise known as the Swann Report, could be mistaken for a sentence from the 1999 *Commission of Inquiry Report into the Murder of Stephen Lawrence.* Both documents are seminal works of their times, holding up a mirror to reflect a British society that, while tolerant on the outside, is riven with prejudice just beneath the surface. While Swann didn't use the phrase 'institutional racism,' two words that the Macpherson report managed to make a household phrase overnight, that is precisely what he was referring to. Both documents raise awareness of the continuing inequalities in the education system. The Swann Report recommendations were largely ignored by a Conservative government that preferred to generalise race and ethnicity issues as belonging to 'problems' of the inner city. Fourteen years after its publication, the Macpherson report has found it necessary to echo Swann's call for multicultural teaching in the curriculum and an end to overt and covert racism in the education system. While the Department for Education is unlikely to adapt the national curriculum beyond, possibly, including guidance on multiculturalism in the proposed citizenship syllabus, it will be interesting to see how the education establishment responds to Macpherson's recommendations.

What does all this have to do with disaffection? Look at the facts in Britain today.

- Black boys are four to six times, and in some areas up to fifteen times more likely than white counterparts to be excluded.

- Few schools or education authorities analyse exclusion data in terms of ethnicity; neither do they acknowledge racist provocation that leads black children to react in ways that lead to their exclusion.

- African Caribbean pupils are the lowest performing group at GCSE level, with 9% leaving school without a single exam, as compared with 6% of whites.

- In 1996, less than a quarter of African Caribbean pupils attained five or more A to C grade GCSEs.

- Bangladeshis and Pakistanis, too, are disproportionately represented in ungraded groups.

- Ethnic minority children are more likely to be bullied than their white peers.

- Teachers' academic expectations of certain minority groups, particularly Bangladeshis, Pakistanis and Gypsy Travellers, are 'unreasonably low.'[1]

- Some schools have stereotypes of African Caribbean pupils' behaviour that have no basis in reality.

- Many schools are reluctant to choose topics in the programmes of study that reflect pupils' cultural and ethnic backgrounds.

- Few schools monitor the curriculum vis a vis raising achievement of ethnic minority pupils.

- While some education authorities actively work towards addressing the under-representation of ethnic minority staff in their schools, others don't.

* As Section 11 grants wither away, schools are finding it increasingly difficult to provide pupils who have English as an additional language with the support they need.

Across the Atlantic, the situation is even more graphic. Four times more Hispanic young people than whites drop out of school: nearly 30% compared to just over 7%. Overall, 62% of Hispanics complete high school, as opposed to 83% of black students and 91.5% of whites. In addition, black and Hispanic boys constitute the overwhelming majority in separate 'special education' classes for disruptive and/or underachieving students in inner city schools.

Whose attitude problem?

What these figures indicate, among other things, is a worrying and substantial gulf between policy and practice. The clarion call for race equality and social inclusion in schools may be sounding loud and clear from both sides of the Atlantic, buttressed by government initiated programmes and policies. But the reality is that on the ground, ethnic minority children continue to grow alienated, bored and frustrated by a system that underestimates their potential, expects them to behave badly in line with racist stereotypes and ignores the different cultural backgrounds that are intrinsic to the way they act and think. If that isn't institutional racism, what is?

Where we go from this position depends on how serious our educational institutions are about addressing race and ethnicity as part of the general fight against disaffection. Teacher training and intensive staff development are central to any change. African American educationalist Crystal Kuykendall refers to studies which conclude that:

> One of the biggest problems in educating these ('multicultural high school dropouts') youth is changing the behaviour of teachers who often erode student confidence and their fragile sense of acceptance of their peers. Students are likely to go to great lengths to avoid teachers who they felt had placed them in uncomfortable or humiliating positions... All too often, there's a reluctance on the teacher's part to use educational programmes or teaching techniques that will yield positive outcomes and enhance student motivation.[2]

Among the factors Kuykendall identifies that influence teachers' attitudes are pupils' previous academic performance. A slow academic start can seal a child's fate in the eyes of teachers who are susceptible to racial stereotyping. The same is true of a child who has demonstrated behaviour that is different to his or her white peers. The particularly ebullient and assertive way that some black children have of expressing themselves can be threatening to white teachers who have no understanding of the culture behind the behaviour and the difference between it and having 'an attitude'.[3] The negativity with which such teachers meet black children's behaviour – over-controlling, punitive – is likely to inhibit the children and, with time, frustrate and demotivate them. A vicious circle is set in train which could end with children being loosely labelled EBD at worst or at best, disruptive. Either way, a child whose behaviour stands out from the norm is likely to attract what behaviour management guru Bill Rodgers calls 'manic vigilance.' By mere dint of ethnic minority children's differentness, they become a problem. And in the present climate in this country, a problematic child is one who could well find themselves excluded at some point or other.

Is it any wonder that as black children go through the education system, their self-image diminishes, step by step? A striking, if old, American study revealed that while 80% of black children began school with healthy self-esteem, only 20% retained it after six years and, by 12th grade, a mere 5% had managed to hold onto it.[4] Certainly in the United States, the tracking system has a lot to answer for, creating a 'caste system' within schools in which black children dominate the lower achievement groups.[5]

How schools can redress the balance

If young people from ethnic minorities are at particular risk of disaffection due, in part, to the myriad manifestations of institutional racism that surround them in our society, schools must take the lead by adapting the curriculum and school ethos to the culturally diverse populations that they serve and do so creatively and sensitively. An illuminating British study of 48 schools undertaken by Ofsted as a follow-up to its highly critical 1996 review of research on the achievement of ethnic minority pupils by Gillborn and Gipps highlights the continuing deficits but also the patches of good practice that exist. It makes some positive recommendations on how schools can better support and encourage ethnic minority pupils. Although not targeted at dropout prevention, the following suggestions contribute to a climate that nurtures, encourages, motivates and stimulates all children and particularly those at risk. Bear in mind that the Ethnic Minority Achievement Grant has superceded Section 11, widening the remit beyond exclusive language support. Among the recommendations:

- First and foremost, create an early warning system by monitoring pupil performance by ethnicity. That way, if underachievement is evident, an analysis of the reasons for it can be undertaken and training and resources directed appropriately. 'Ignorance of what lies behind underachievement... fuels prejudice and stereotypical attitudes towards minority groups...'[6]

- Similarly, exclusions and attendance should be monitored in terms of ethnicity and analyses undertaken to look at the causes of exclusion and school absences.

- Introduce policies and strategies aimed at raising teacher expectation of minority ethnic pupils, including: in-service training on assessment, behaviour management, recording and reporting, meetings with all teaching staff to formulate appropriate expectations for each year group.

- Organise children in mixed ethnic and gender groups in the classroom.

- Raise Section 11 teachers' status and effectiveness by focusing language support work on the curriculum and formalising teaching partnerships with class teachers.

- Develop home/school liaison with Section 11 teachers who preferably come from the community or have close knowledge of it.

- Set clear targets, establish monitoring of academic outcomes by ethnicity, ensuring equal opportunities policies extend to award-giving ceremonies.

- Ensure that the curriculum reflects the pupils' cultural backgrounds by choosing relevant areas of work from the programmes of study. Encourage cross-curricular multiculturalism and develop policies that emphasise positive images of ethnic minorities in the curriculum. Share multicultural projects, issues and themes with parents and the wider community.

- To help children with English as an additional language, increase oral work in the classroom and allow for more collaborative acitivites. Providing an extra English option gives extra language support to pupils who need it.

- Develop a pastoral care system that is sensitive and responsive to all children, including those from ethnic minorities.

- If Traveller children attend the school, ensure close collaboration between teaching staff and the LEA Traveller Education Service and awareness of issues facing Traveller children by the whole staff.

- Develop carefully planned, sustainable mentoring schemes involving community and business partnerships as well as peer projects

- Offer study support activities after school with appropriate staffing.

- Involve parents in the life of the school by offering activities (eg computer classes, literacy programmes, parentcraft and childcare courses) and ensuring that all communications are translated into community languages. Encourage parents to participate in children's homework and project work by sending out translated material and/or running after-school curriculum workshops and meetings.

- To support the equal opportunities policy, a review of all school policies and procedures should be undertaken to ascertain whether ethnic minority pupils are discriminated against in any way.

- LEAs must creatively tackle the issue of recruiting ethnic minority teachers.

On a one to one basis, teachers have enormous powers to motivate the disaffected black pupil. Goal-setting and rewarding pupils when they've achieved their aims is a simple behaviour modification technique that is effective, no matter what the age. It also helps to create role models from peers, thereby challenging any anti-achievement culture that exists in the school. Outside role models from pupils' cultures should also be made use of, from historical and international figures to contemporary professionals and popular icons. Carefully chosen mentors from the pupils' community can have a powerful motivating impact. Regular feedback on pupils' goals, preferably in one to one sessions, gives pupils the message that the teacher is concerned with their progress and is encouraging them in their aims. Identifying and maximising pupils' strengths is another great motivator, raising children's self-esteem and allowing teachers to build on their aptitudes.

Diversifying pedagogy

At the heart of it all is an attempt to understand where these children are coming from, metaphorically speaking. Kuykendall talks about the need for teachers to have a knowledge and acceptance of the 'stage setting' that black young people often engage in before getting down to a classroom assignment. This is played out in ways that look a lot like disruptive procrastination, ie, asking for directions to be repeated, rearranging themselves in their seats, needing to change pens or get more paper, etc. If teachers know and accept that these rituals will occur and allow a few minutes for them to take place, they will not only avoid confrontation but communicate understanding to their pupils.

The interactive classroom environment is a key component for engaging ethnic minority children as well as non-minority children who aren't academically plugged into school. Stimulating the whole class through active, challenging discussion and through quick-fire demands of answers to questions keeps the adrenaline going. So do experiential activities integrated into lessons and physical activity or movement – well worth the inevitable noise and commotion they will momentarily create. Some of the most exciting, engaging classes I've seen have had African American high school students playing the part of neutrons moving around each other or hamming it up as they act out restaurant scenes in French.

Peer mentoring or tutoring is a particularly powerful tool. Conferring responsibility and status to children whose self-esteems are battered is giving them the unequivocal message that they are valued and important. Even homework assignments can boost self-image when they're cleverly angled to draw on interests that pupils have. If the teacher can make a point of creating regular opportunities for children to succeed at something, pupils' connectedness with their learning, however tenuous, will be sustained. It's not easy to devise such work for clearly non-academic young people, but with a bit of time and ingenuity, assignments can be cooked up that, for instance, have them reflecting on their personal experiences or creating wish-fulfillment scenarios. Everyone has dreams.

In enforcing discipline, a distinction needs to be drawn between the pupil acting out the behaviour and the behaviour itself, to make it clear that although the behaviour itself is not on, the pupil is still accepted as a human being. Fairness is all-important. A pupil who thinks they're being picked on by a teacher because of the colour of their skin or the way they talk is as good as lost to that teacher and possibly to the whole school. One way of demonstrating fairness is by enlisting pupils to collaborate on a behaviour code and helping to enforce it. By sharing this important decision-making process and entrusting them to see that rules are followed, the them-and-us culture is broken down. They take ownership over the smooth running of the class.

Reaching out, drawing in

Community organisations are another part of the picture, having an important part to play in acting as a bridge between black and ethnic minority families and the school. Saturday schools run by African Caribbean community groups have long been doing tremendous work in raising achievement and motivation of children who may be floundering or are disinterested. While it shouldn't be up to outside groups to be educating children in the basics and giving them a sense of their own culture and history, when these things aren't happening in mainstream schools, the Saturday schools have been determined to fill the breach themselves. There are also black parents' organsations who liaise with schools on behalf of families when necessary, for instance over disputed exclusions.

Finally, positive interaction with parents is a crucial issue. In Crystal Kuykendall's professional experience, 'many black and Hispanic parents to whom I've spoken have expressed dismay over the condescending and pedantic tone of some classroom teachers'. Any parent, black or white, who has had meetings with teachers will be sensitive to nuance, body language and use of terminology when their children are under discussion and particularly when they know their children have problems at school. When the parents are black or ethnic minority and most if not all of the teachers are white, those sensitivities will be even more acute. Racial stereotypes and preconceptions about single parent and/or low income families will taint the relationship between teacher and parent forever. All teachers know how important it is to work with parents in order to boost children's achievement and improve behaviour and attitude. There can be no effective partnership without respect and trust on both sides.

The underachievement, disengagement and exclusion rates of black young people in the British school system is not a new phenomenon. In the 1970s we had the scandal of African Caribbean boys being labelled 'ESN'.[7] Today, they are being labelled EBD or disruptive and being excluded. It is part of a continuum of mismatched perceptions, mutual distrust and breakdown of communication that exists in some but by no means all schools. While the Macpherson report has been a great asset in jolting consciousness in all areas of our society, schools included, about the ways our institutions work against minorities, it will be the way schools redefine themselves to be socially inclusive environments that will, in the final analysis, put an end to the educational disenfranchisement of young black people.

References

1. *Raising the attainment of minority ethnic pupils*, Ofsted, 1999.

2. Kuykendall, C. *From Rage to Hope: Reclaiming Black and Hispanic Students*, National Educational Service, 1991.

3. The attitude of white teachers to African Caribbean boys is described by Tony Sewell in his *Black Maculinities and Schooling: How Black Boys Survive Modern Schooling*, Trentham, 1997.

4. Silberman, C. *Crisis in the Classroom*, Vintage Books, 1971.

5. Rist, R. 'Study of how teachers treat children differently' in Final Report on *The Schooling of Young Children: Cognitive and Affective Outcomes*, US National Institute of Education, 1978.

6. *Raising the attainment of minority ethnic pupils, op cit.*

7. Coard, B. *How the West Indian Child is made Educationally Subnormal in the British School System*. New Beacon Books, 1971

CHAPTER FIVE

THE UGLY AMERICAN STATE OF EDUCATION: HOME OF THE BEST AND THE WORST

America is a land of dreams and nightmares, of aspirations and disappointments, of streets paved with gold and other streets ingrained with the detritus of hopelessness. It is a land where the rich have their own security guards and where there are public housing projects containing 55,000 people, all of them afraid to go out after dark. It is a land where the sick and well-off stay in hospitals that look like four star hotels and where the sick and poor can't afford to go to the doctor. It is a land containing the richest people on the planet who got there by looking after number one. And it is where the poor, many of them, have given up on finding justice in the world. It is a microcosm of all societies, good and bad, self-seeking and altruistic. As the most diverse of countries it is the most accepting of difference – and the most prejudiced against it. It has been said many times before: America is a land of extremes.

Educational apartheid

Nowhere are the paradigms of those extremes more visible than in the nation's schools. Where the white and affluent send their children to well-resourced public schools or else private schools, many inner city public schools attended by poor white, black and ethnic minority children look like what you would expect in the developing world. Jonathan Kozol's impassioned book on the degradation of America's inner city schools, *Savage Inequalities*, brought home the realities of the apartheid public education system to white, middle class, private school-educated America for the first time. A former teacher, Kozol visited schools around the country after a break of 25 years and found ...

extraordinarily unhappy places. With few exceptions, they re-
minded me of 'garrisons' or 'outposts' in a foreign nation. Housing projects, bleak and tall, surrounded by perimeter walls lined
with barbed wire, often stood adjacent to the schools... Doors were
guarded. Police sometimes patrolled the halls. The windows of the
schools were often covered with steel grates... Looking around
some of these inner-city schools, where filth and disrepair were
worse than anything I'd seen in 1964, I often wondered why we
would agree to let our children go to school in places where no
politician, school board president or business CEO would dream of
working.[1]

Kozol's description of these schools, where even the most basic resources such as books and adequate heating are lacking, is among the
most chilling indictments ever to emerge of a system that is founded on
inequality.

The funding system for state schools itself sets the agenda. Under the
foundation programme system, by which public (state) schools are
funded, local people pay taxes based on the value of their homes and
businesses. In prosperous districts, this local tax is sufficient to run
their schools. In poorer areas, less money will be raised because
property is worth less. So each state is required to top up the poorer districts' funds, ostensibly making them level with the richest districts.
But in reality, the states only top up funds to a level that will ensure the
schools are able to provide a minimum education – considerably lower
than what is found in wealthier areas. As Kozol puts it:

It guarantees that every child has 'an equal minimum' but not that
every child has the same. Stated in a slightly different way, it
guarantees that every child has a building called 'a school' but not
that what is found within one school will bear much similarity, if
any, to that which is found in another.[2]

Under this system, the disparities of funding between school districts
are glaring. New York City area figures for school funding show a discrepancy of nearly $8,000 on annual spending per pupil between the
wealthier suburbs of Westchester County and the inner city. Even with
special Title I federal top-up funding for schools in disadvantaged
areas, the contrasts remain.

US dropout rates: a national scandal

Across the country, public schools watch impotently as failing students drop off the edge, get up and walk out the door forever. Nationally, an average of one quarter of all eighth graders (aged 13) fail to graduate high school. In some areas, the situation is much worse. In New York City and Washington DC, the figure is a staggering 45% and in Dayton, Ohio, an average midwestern town no worse and no better than many, half of all high school students drop out. Overall, this means that one child out of every four in the United States leave school without that most basic of American necessities, a high school diploma.

What these figures communicate is that 'traditional schools are only serving 75% of students at most,' in the words of Dr Jay Smink, director of the National Dropout Prevention Center in South Carolina. The remainder will be cast adrift without another necessity for the outside world: self-esteem. A large number of drop-outs will have been held back two grades, ensuring that their self-image is truly at ground zero, before they decide to call it a day, The likelihood of them drifting into drug abuse and crime is high.

While the figures are worse than in the UK, the risk factors for US drop-outs are not dissimilar to those in Britain. They include: living in high-growth areas, living in unstable school districts, having parents who aren't high school graduates, speaking English as a second language, having negative self-perceptions, being bored or alienated, having low self-esteem and working (boys) and having a child (girls).[3]

So what is there to look to America for? Plenty. With the realisation that the system has hit rock bottom has also come the understanding that radical change is the only way forward. Traditional approaches to underachievement – reducing class sizes, holding children back a grade, setting – haven't made an impact in themselves. In fact, the latter two have been proved to be particularly counterproductive. A number of different kinds of schools have been introduced and become part of the education landscape in an attempt both to widen parent choice and to stem the tide of failure. Some of them have created new pedagogies. Others have decided to defy received wisdom and raise the standards and expectations of kids destined for failure to dizzying new heights – and have succeeded.

The importance of being emotionally literate

Before looking at some of those schools, let's take a detour to look at the problem of disaffection from a different angle, one that is being used around the United States in various guises and is beginning to take hold in Britain on a smaller, more fragmented scale. It's called social and emotional learning, or social development. As a model of education meeting the needs of its disadvantaged, at-risk community, it is the most holistic in concept in that in its ideal form it is early intervention, from the very point of a child's entry into the education system. Although not specifically described as drop-out prevention, it has a positive effect on students' motivation to learn as well as many other things including boosting self-esteem and communication skills. The focus is not on conventional, academic learning but on engendering social and emotional intellligence in children.

Without it, says Daniel Goleman in his ground-breaking, inter-nationally best-selling book, *Emotional Intelligence*, we can't achieve our full potential because we're unable to translate our cognitive abilities into language, relationships, behaviour, self-image and emotional stability. His theory came as a clarion call to the education world. People, he maintains, can have high IQs, but without 'EQ' – emotional intelligence – they can't function fully as friends, as lovers, as communicators, as managers, as team workers, as individual achievers. He defines emotional intelligence as

> *abilities such as being able to motivate oneself and persist in the face of frustrations; to control impulse and delay gratification; to regulate one's moods and keep distress from swamping the ability to think; to empathise and to hope.*

Underlining his point, Goleman quotes Professor Howard Gardner, author of *Multiple Intelligences*: 'In the day to day world, no intelligence is more important than the interpersonal. If you don't have it, you'll make poor choices about who to marry, what job to take and so on. We need to train children in the personal intelligences in school.'[4]

As I sit writing this, President Clinton has called on schools to teach children to deal with their violent feelings in the wake of the shooting of thirteen high school students at Columbine High School in a suburb of Denver. They were killed by two of their classmates, who have been described as disaffected. White, bright and middle class, they none-theless were outsiders in a school where cliques ruled and where their esoteric, non-conformist style made them the butts of physical and verbal bullying. Alienated and hurt, they retaliated by immersing them-selves in a cobbled together hate and death culture that reached its apotheosis on Hitler's birthday, 1999 and ended in their own suicides.

Eric Harris and Dylan Klebold are as unrepresentative of the many thousands of troubled youth in the United States as they are of the estimated one million teenagers who carry guns to school to 'defend themselves' every day. But what they had in common with other at-risk youth was their difficulty in understanding and communicating their emotions. Behind their weird, trenchcoated veneers, they were as inscrutable to themselves as they were to the outside world and even, reportedly, their parents.

President Clinton's demand comes too late for Columbine High, but may help reduce the nearly half a million incidents of violence or criminal acts that take place every year in American schools. What he's calling for is no mean feat but neither is it beyond the capability of well-organised and committed schools to deliver: in a nutshell, the teaching of emotional literacy to the nation's children.

As with gun legislation, tough action has to be taken and Clinton is rightly striking while the iron's hot. There has been no better time for the government to federally mandate that every school in the land pre-sent a full curriculum that contains the skills needed for children to understand themselves and get on with each other in different relation-ships, in different contexts. To have any real impact, it must operate from kindergarten through to twelfth grade, not as an add-on but as a mandatory subject, in a developmentally appropriate programme. It should be a carefully researched curriculum that works to engender 'communication skills, self awareness, empathy, managing emotions, handling relationships and how to motivate oneself'.[5] It is only by em-bedding these skills and understandings into schools that the dis-affected of the future, whether they're bright like Dylan Kiebold and Eric Harris of Columbine High School or not so bright, can hope to acquire the resiliency to deal with the many blows that life throws at them.

We in Britain need it, too. We need to have it embedded in the national curriculum as part of a new, revamped, prioritised Personal Social and Health Education syllabus. And the new education action zones, which have the freedom to take radical measures, need to have it integrated as fully as possible into the entire curriculum in a bold attempt to reverse the low self-esteem, low expectations and low academic outcomes of children in disadvantaged areas. This entails bottom-up training and on-going staff development to shift attitudes and learn new skills, to break down barriers and raise awareness in teachers of the expressions of cultural diversity in all its guises and many of the finer points of child development that have been dispensed with in training over the past few years. To not grasp the nettle at this turning point, when change and innovation is there for the taking, and when the consequences of not doing so are so sickeningly stark, is nothing less than perverse.

A haven of emotional intelligence

A good place to look for a model of how it's done is New Haven, Connecticut where, since 1990, social and emotional learning has been part of the statutory curriculum for all children. It is the only school district in the country to have implemented such a programme of learn-ing. It is not an add-on. Once or twice weekly circle time would not suffice for the rigorous thinkers, movers and shakers behind the pro-gramme. When New Haven's superintendent of schools saw the writing on the wall, he knew he had to take radical, structural action.

In the 1980s, the youth of New Haven were in big trouble. Despite being home to Yale, one of the two most prestigious universities in the United States, New Haven is the fourth poorest city in the country and had one of the highest drop-out rates, with half of all 14 year olds fail-ing to graduate high school. Last decade, it also had the dubious distinction of having the fourth highest teenage pregnancy rate nationally and similarly alarming rates of drug abuse among the young. In the late 1980s, there were forty five youth gang-related homicides a year. 'For awhile,' says Captain Francisco Ortiz of the New Haven police department, 'it was difficult for kids to go to school. We've got metal detectors in the schools today because the kids asked for them.'

These grim facts led the superintendent to call together a large team of educationalists, academics from Yale, parents and community and religious leaders to look at why New Haven children were falling off the edge and what the school district could do about it.

They first set themselves the task of identifying personality traits common to the drop-outs, teenage mothers and drug users. They found that these young people lacked impulse control, they were poor at stress management, problem solving and decision making, they had low self-esteem and poor communication skills, they had trouble understanding people different to themselves and they had little grasp of values like justice and friendship.

The experts then got down to work designing a curriculum that would address these issues, from kindergarten through to twelfth grade, in a way that would be developmentally appropriate for each year group. At Yale's psychology department, a national search was conducted for curricula already in existence that worked on specific competencies that related to these deficits. Then special committees for each grade level moulded the curricular models to meet the needs of New Haven children.

The result is that since 1990, the social development programme, as it's called, has been taught as a discrete subject in all elementary and middle schools and is integrated as much as possible into the school day. The curriculum teaches children skills required for decision-making, peer relationships, problem-solving, resisting drugs and alcohol, stress management, self-control, violence prevention and sexuality. Teaching strategies range from role play to stories, games and activities to discussion.

Take the example of Project Charlie, a syllabus specifically designed for problem-solving that is used with kindergartners up to third graders (5 to 8 year olds) as part of the social development programme curriculum. It is an interactive approach that teaches children to take responsibility for their behaviour by talking problems through as they arise and thinking about solutions and their consequences. It helps them to find ways of handling anger, frustration and disappointment by validating those feelings, using the model of a traffic light to positively channel them. When something happens to upset you, you go through the colours of the traffic light. Red means stop and cool down. Yellow is wait and think about the problem. The green light is go: talk about it .

The specially trained elementary and middle school teachers carry the programme lessons through into other areas effortlessly. In an English lesson, a third grade teacher I observed read a story to her class about a little girl sitting and eating her breakfast when suddenly her cat jumps on her and causes juice to spill all over her shirt. 'How can she get rid of her anger?' asked the teacher. They children were all desperate to answer, with variations on the theme of using her voice to reprimand the cat, after she's stopped, thought about it and allowed herself to cool down a bit.

New Haven's model isn't perfect. Despite earlier plans to implement a curriculum at high school level, this hasn't happened due to management problems and curricular constraints. Still, there is a peer leadership programme in operation which has a self-selected group of volunteers in the twelfth grade (18 year olds in their final year of high school) running sex education and violence and dropout prevention sessions with tenth and eleventh graders.

Far-reaching results

Research shows that the New Haven programme has helped to bring about significant improvements in students' behaviour and academic attainment. The Social and Health Assessment report carried out every two years by the school district reveals that between 1992 and 1996, the numbers of sixth graders having to repeat a grade was reduced by 10%. Attainment in the Connecticut Mastery Tests, the state's standardised tests for fourth, sixth and eighth graders in verbal and non-verbal skills have improved yearly. For instance, 41% of fourth graders achieved a standard of good or excellent in 1993; in 1997, the figure had leapt to 72%. There was an eight per cent drop in the numbers of 12 year olds who said they had sex. And dropout rates, suspensions and exclusions have all fallen. In addition, the numbers of children carrying guns to school dropped by one half and there was a nine per cent decrease in knives being carried to school.

While nobody would claim that these improvements are all down to the programme, teachers and programme facilitators are convinced that it has made a significant impact on students' behaviour, attitude and attainment. The principal of Welch Annexe Elementary School, Gina Wells, said:

If you could take my children and put them together with others who hadn't had this programme, I'd say they'd have higher scores. I believe they're better equipped to read and write because of this programme. But the reality is that we've got fifteen 5 to 7 year olds on Prozac, Ritalin (for attention deficit disorder) and anti-psychotic drugs. I've got one 7 year old here who's been sexually abused half a dozen times and others whose fathers are in jail. So my main focus isn't on raising achievement. What we're doing is empowering children to make the right decisions.[6]

New Haven is a singular example of a school district that has seen the abyss and, through a collaboration between community and academics, has come up with a radical and pedagogically sound strategy to strengthen children's defences against it.

Different models of schools

There are many other social development programmes around the United States that, while not mandated by an entire school district to run throughout a child's school life, are delivered in a bid to prioritise children's emotional literacy.

Far more widespread are different models of schools. Whether created in response to disaffection or answering the insatiable clamour for diversity in education, America is in the grip of a proliferation of less conventionally structured schools, spread around the country. Each school within each category is different, but all fit into these general descriptions.

Magnet schools

Magnet schools, state-run specialty schools that focus on specific academic areas or arts, have tripled in number in ten years and have proved to be successful in raising achievement. There are magnet schools for the performing arts, for science, for technology, etc. Their name reflects the fact that they attract children from different areas, and they make possible racial mixing where black and white children may not have been educated together before. As America enters a new era in which legislation introduced in the 1960s to desegregate schools is being overturned in one state after another, magnet schools may become the only racially integrated schools.

Charter schools

Charter schools are newer, more radical in concept and spreading like wildfire. A cross between public and private school, they are set up by parents, teachers or community organisations who have a vision of a different kind of school. They secure state funding by entering a contractual agreement – or charter – with the school district to achieve an agreed level for state academic standards and federal regulations within three years, or else their charter is revoked and they have to close. This is matched, by and large, with corporate funding. How they achieve their agreed targets, set at a reasonably high level, is up to them: they have full autonomy from the school district. The fact that they're deregulated is part of the great attraction of these schools for some – and the source of major controversy for others. They can have certain rules and regulations waived, such as not having to hire certified teachers and not following the state curriculum in the same way that mainstream schools are required to do.

They represent a wide range of approaches, styles and methodologies, some of them novel. The Youth Build Philadelphia Charter School, for instance, combines academic, work-related and leadership training to prepare students for the transition to the world of work. The curriculum is focused on rehabilitating old buildings. Magellan Charter School in North Carolina serves a number of pupils considered academically gifted. Classes of no more than fifteen are taught by parent volunteers. The Museum School is a partnership between the Children's Museum of San Diego and the City School District that uses museum resources and those of other cultural institutions to deliver an interdisciplinary curriculum. Skyview School in Arizona calls itself a Multiple Intelligence School 'dedicated to helping children learn in a variety of ways.' A school of 127 children, it was founded by parents and educators and emphasises parents' role in the learning experience. It operates on a modified calendar and groups its kindergarten to 14 year olds in multi-age groups. In San Rafael in northern California, the Sobriety High School sounds exactly what it is: a school for those at risk of or already experiencing 'chemical dependency problems.' It's run by a partnership between the Marin County Office of Education, social services and judicial agencies.

Charter schools are gaining a reputation for innovation, although because they are so new, no evaluations exist. But that they are controversial and will remain so for a long time to come, there's no doubt. One circuit court judge in the state of Michigan declared them unconstitutional because although they were run as private schools, they were funded on taxpayers' money.[7] Still, they are the hottest thing on the education reform circuit at the moment, growing in number in just five years to about 700 today and catering for 170,000 young students, many of them at risk.

Alternative high schools

I will be documenting two schools that fall into yet another category: alternative high schools. Each of the 15,000 school districts in the United States has some form of alternative programme. Many have more than one. Originally conceived as a radical departure from formalised, structured, institutional environments, they were test beds of experimentation drawing from British models including A.S. Neill's Summerhill and also from vertically grouped open classrooms in the state primary schools. Their genesis in the late 60s and early 70s was conceptually far removed from what they have become. Today, they have been transformed beyond recognition to become something more along the lines of Pupil Referral Units in the UK, last chance high schools catering specifically for pupils who have been excluded or are at risk of dropping out. Some young people are referred by their high schools and others refer themselves. Because there are some very creative, very committed people working in the field of alternative education, these schools vary widely in structure, ethos and scope. Some fall into the realms of the proverbial sin bin, some are renowned for being free and easy and therefore ineffectual. And a small number of others, including the ones I have chosen to look at, are models of dynamic practice that are literally turning their pupils' lives around – and have the figures to prove it – by bringing a new radicalism to alternative education: high expectations.

Alternative education is known as dropout prevention. There are three basic forms that it takes:

* a free standing alternative high school that serves a local catchment area, usually housed in a disused and down at heel building owned

by the school district. Some are able to keep class sizes very small, others are indistinguishable from ordinary classes. But generally, the student population is much smaller than mainstream schools, numbering a few hundred at most;

- programmes run within a school, in a bid to keep the students within a mainstream environment. The idea is that students share facilities and, with time, will be re-integrated into the larger school;

- middle college high schools, first pioneered in 1974. Here, an alternative high school is located on a college or junior college campus, enabling at-risk students to be surrounded by positive role models, including large numbers of their own ethnicity, and to share state of the art facilities. Under this system, pupils are allowed to take college courses alongside junior college students if they reach a certain standard in their own curriculum. As with the other examples of alternative education, teachers combine strong pastoral support with academic instruction.

In the next chapter, I'll be looking at two free-standing alternative high schools that are proving that these particular last chance highs are giving the young and at risk the academic skills and self-esteem they need to turn themselves around. Although not mainstream schools, their ethos and practice offer much that British educationalists working in many sectors can learn from.

References

1. Kozol, J. *Savage Inequalities*, HarperPerennial, 1992.
2. Kozol, *ibid.*
3. Druian, G. *et al, Effective Schooling Practices and At Risk Youth: What the Research Shows*, The Northwest Regional Educational Laboratory, part of the US Department of Education's Office of Educational Research and Improvement, 1997.
4. Goleman, D. *Emotional Intelligence*, Bantam Books, 1995.
5. Peter Salovey's definition of emotional intelligence in D. Goleman's *Emotional Intelligence, ibid.*
6. *Times Educational Supplement*, July 10, 1998.
7. *School Choice and Charter Schools*, National Conference of State Legislatures, 1995.

CHAPTER SIX

THE ALCHEMISTS: SCHOOLS RECLAIMING THE ALIENATED

T his chapter describes in depth two schools in very different parts of the United States, chosen because of their proven success and the distinctively different approaches they've adopted to tackle the widespread disaffection that has taken hold of their communities. Both are alternative schools. But they aren't being documented for the excitingly innovative methodologies they use.

There are others that are far more innovative than Hostos Lincoln Academy of Science and Jefferson County High School. But innovation for its own sake means very little if it has no positive impact and many of these more unconventional approaches are too new to have been independently assessed. The schools I document below have been chosen because they are different from the norm in undramatic but important ways and, most crucially, because they produce outcomes that leave their mainstream counterparts out in the cold.

I've also chosen these models for the vision that drives them – something that I would call a humanistic realism. Whether in the ghettoes of New York City or down in Kentucky, the educationalists driving these schools have a belief in the potential of the young and disaffected to not only rise above their difficulties, some of which almost defy belief, but to reclaim a future for themselves based on high aspirations and hard work. While researching these schools in the United States, I heard stories of young people who had grown up in the worst conditions imaginable winding up as teachers, lawyers, doctors, entrepreneurs, writers and musicians, in large part because teachers took it upon themselves to wage a Faustian battle for their souls and minds – and won.

Visiting these schools and talking to students and teachers was an un-forgettable experience for me. I met kids whose parents were either absent, dead or dysfunctional because of Aids or other illnesses or drugs, kids who had the responsibility for looking after themselves and sometimes other family members heaped on their young shoulders. I met young people who had suffered abuse, expulsion from their home country, who had been on the brink, because of emotional upset, of drifting into a nihilistic wilderness in which nothing had meaning or value, least of all education. And I heard these young people – African American, Haitian, Dominican, Puerto Rican, white middle class and working class – talk about what their schools had come to mean to them. For many, it was the centre of their existence, the one safe refuge in their chaotic lives, their lifeline to normality. For all of them, it was quite simply their salvation.

The stories of how these schools have given young people back their desire to achieve has lessons for everyone concerned with making education relevant and responsive to those whose material, social and emotional problems stand in the way of their learning.

Hostos Lincoln Academy of Science, New York City

If there's a single district in the whole of the United States that is synonymous with violence, crime, social disorganisation and ingrained deprivation, it must be the South Bronx. In its mean streets, over-shadowed by brooding public housing tower blocks as far as the eye can see and liquor stores that wouldn't look out of place in the slums of Soweto or Tijuana, it is the quintessential symbol of urban decay at the fag end of the 20th century.

Situated in the Bronx, one of New York City's five boroughs, the South Bronx's notoriety has been enhanced, if not immortalised, by the 1981 film 'Fort Apache,' set in the neighbourhood of Hunts Point. In the film, Paul Newman is a good cop battling against corruption, violent crime, drugs and the desperation of poverty in one of the grimmest corners of New York, if not the universe.

During my time in the South Bronx, within shooting distance of Fort Apache, I'm sad to say I saw no one remotely resembling Paul New-man. In fact, I saw very few white people apart from a few vagrants.

But I did hear police sirens shrieking past with regularity that I admit to finding vaguely comforting, reminding me as they did of my own Hackney neighbourhood.

I saw all around me human reminders that this is the poorest congressional district in the whole of the United States: the down and outs on the street, many of them looking like victims of care in the community, that most cynical of exercises which, like so many others, the British borrowed from America; the young and not so young, clearly bombed out of their heads as they careered down the street; and ordinary working class New Yorkers, mostly Hispanic and African American, going about their business, working, shopping, picking up their children.

New York City is not so much a melting pot as an overstuffed cauldron teeming with all the nationalities of the world, and the Bronx is a concentrated version of it – after all the wealthier nations have been gently lifted out of the strainer and despatched elsewhere. The tired and the poor, refugees and migrant workers legal and otherwise, working minority families, mainly headed by single mothers: all seem to have somehow made their way to the South Bronx. It hardly needs pointing out, such is the way of the world and certainly the way of the New York education system, that this isn't an area renowned for its schools. One local high school, John F. Kennedy, has over 5,000 students on its rolls.

Smack in the middle of this jam-packed multicultural hodge podge of neediness, on the once grand thoroughfare of Grand Concourse, sits Hostos Community College, a junior college that is part of the City University of New York. It serves a mainly ethnic minority student population destined for university or vocational training. And within this security-guarded, modern, glassy building is housed yet another educational institution of a very different kind. Here, on the third and fourth floors, there's little glass – or in fact any windows to speak of in most of the classrooms, which bear an uncanny similarity to fluorescent-lit concrete bunkers. There are great gaping holes in the plaster and the floors have clearly seen better decades. But in this unlovely space inhabited by Hostos Lincoln Academy of Science (HLAS), academic alchemy is taking place every day. Flying in the face of reality, Hostos Lincoln is transforming kids once classified as potential drop-outs into high school graduates with high aspirations.

HLAS is a small alternative high school, one of 75 run by New York City Board of Education, serving students who their previous schools have given up on – and vice versa. It caters for 325 students at risk of dropping out, most of them referred by their mainstream schools because of underachievement, bad behaviour, truancy and expulsions. No less than 98% are from ethnic minorities, mainly Hispanic, with 22% African Americans; the rest are for the most part Asian immigrants and refugees from the Balkans. Three quarters are entitled to free school lunch, which in American social welfare terms means that they are living below the poverty line.

A boy-less landscape

From the moment I walked into the school, I felt there was something odd about it. Here's a school for disaffected students and all the figures show that boys far outnumber girls in truancy and disruptive behaviour figures. But at Hostos, 85% of the students are female. Dr Michele Cataldi, founder and principal of HLAS, offers me his starkly succinct and depressing assessment of why this is when I ask him where the boys are. 'In this community, boys are falling off the edge.' Boys drop out and proceed to get their education on the streets or in prison. They achieve status zero with alarming speed and ease. In these neighbourhoods of the South Bronx, school is for girls.

This being so, these ghetto girls are for learning. They are, for the most part, students who at their previous schools were more drop-ins than drop-outs: they attended school regularly but were quiet, withdrawn, disengaged. They didn't act out so much as opt out in their seats – the ones who so easily fall through the cracks without being noticed. But at Hostos Lincoln, staff and students put the past behind them. Previous failures are irrelevant. Founder and principal Dr Michele Cataldi, an effervescent Italian with a melting pot of an accent runs a ship that is tight but generous, with high standards and equally high commitment of staff to get their students achieving.

> In thirty years of working with disaffected children, I've seen alternative high schools where the staff lowered expectations and standards. But I realised that it's not as it should be. We should be bringing students to our level instead of lowering ourselves to theirs. Young people don't want to be your buddy and call you by

your first name. They want to be safe and to know that what they're doing for the six or seven hours they spend in school everyday has value and meaning.

An alternative to alternative schools

One of the fundamental differences between the twelve year old HLAS and other alternative high schools is that its approach is based on early intervention. Rather than starting in the first year of high school – the tenth grade – when they're likely to have already experienced alienation and failure, Hostos students start one year earlier, before their transition from middle to high school, when they're 14 years old. To help with that change, they attend a summer programme preceding their first semester to become acquainted with the school and staff and to get used to the different pitch of things. They come to Hostos from a number of different sources, but mainly either by being referred by their middle schools or by parents' self-referral, based on the positive word of mouth and publicity that are by-products of the school's success.

Another big difference is that where other alternative high schools in the city have customarily used a curriculum designed for less academic students, Hostos puts its students through the demanding Regents curriculum and exams that are used by all mainstream, including private, schools. Explains Cataldi:

Many students from alternative high schools were not succeeding. There was no depth to their knowledge. They've used untraditional methods that are less structured and their outcomes have been similar to each other, generally low. Part of our alternative was to create a more traditional model with a strong academic emphasis.

So traditional is the school curriculum and the stress on academic excellence that the superintendent of alternative high schools once called Hostos 'a throwback to the '50s'.

Unfashionable in alternative education circles as it may be, Hostos Lincoln's traditionalism and emphasis on creating a secure and safe environment have been strong selling points to parents of its largely Hispanic and female intake. The environment, housed as it is within a well-resourced and guarded college, is a far cry from the blackboard jungles containing thousands of unwilling inmates that is the norm in New York City.

Not that Hostos' mainly female students have been cosseted from the vicissitudes of life in the ghetto. As Vicky Sanacore, one of HLAS's veteran teachers, describes it:

These are students who've just arrived to this country with language acquisition problems or come from English as second language homes. We have latchkey children, many living with grandparents or relatives who've adopted them for many reasons ranging from their parents having died of Aids to parents being too strung out on drugs to look after them. Most come from single parent families, a lot of them with mothers working at night cleaning office buildings in the city.

There are exceptions. Alvin Torres' daughter Melissa, now 18, graduated from HLAS in 1998. She had previously gone to a private Catholic elementary school and Torres and his wife were looking for a public school that was safe and small:

She wasn't having problems in school before. But we knew our daughter well enough to know that she'd benefit from a smaller school that presented challenges that would have to be met. Friends mentioned this school to us. When you first hear the words 'alternative high school' you think it's for rejects. But when we came for an interview, we were impressed with how Hostos gave its students oppportunities to become mature and exercise their responsibilities and with the great effort teachers put into helping the students in all the subject areas. Here it wasn't just a matter of giving them homework and leaving the onus on them. Teachers walk through the curriculum with students. Some children have their problems but they also seem to have a genuine desire to move on because the school communicates to them a sense of respect that motivates them. It says 'hey, we're here for you and we're going to help you.' A child who doesn't make it at Hostos really has to work hard not to make it.

Melissa is now at college. She wants to be a child advocacy lawyer and looks destined to achieve her goals. The Torres' younger daughter, also a good student, will be coming to Hostos next year.

Impressive by any standards

People like the Torres' are allured not just by the smallness, security and supportiveness of the school but by the school's exam results and attendance rates which, for an alternative school, are nothing short of surprising and for any school in the Bronx are truly phenomenal. The *New York Times'* league tables of all schools in the state of New York put Hostos Lincoln in the top ten of those adjusted for factors such as income and English language proficiency. Despite the fact that it has on its rolls over 20% more students living on or below the poverty line than the average for New York City, the school had over 20% more students passing their Regents exams than the city average (which takes into account selective schools). Drop-out rates are similarly impressive. Where city-wide the rate is 30% of all students, at HLAS it's 0.3%. And these, remember, are students who were at risk of failing or discontinuing their education.

Schools on both sides of the Atlantic might look to this unprepossessing little establishment suspended in the murky skies overlooking Yankee Stadium as a model of how to motivate and engage the reluctant or troubled learner.

Small, safe, supportive

One of the fundamental features of the school is that it is small and made even smaller by dividing students into family groups of 18 or so, which they remain in with the same teacher for the four years they attend the school. Each family group meets once a day for a session that is partly used to deliver a curriculum of social and life skills and general knowledge not covered in other parts of the curriculum and part informal counselling and sounding off. Teacher Vicky Sanacore, who designed the programme, combined the two elements because, she believes, without specific subject areas such as goal setting, college preparation and American government to give the sessions a focus and a structure, there was always the risk of them being too free-ranging. Synthesising the two creates a forum for airing views, gripes and personal experiences as well as providing a special area of the curriculum for acquiring skills and knowledge that will help them in college and/or the workplace.

Just as crucial to the way the school operates is the level of nurturing and support that each student gets outside the family groups. Good alternative high schools are renowned for ploughing energy and time into boosting students' self-respect. At Hostos, there is similar emphasis on positive reinforcement and a caring ethos, but always buttressed with the drive to succeed academically. Vicky explains:

What's different about our school is that we are committed to making our students feel that they're 'normal,' that they're going to any school in the United States, that they can take any class they want to take and pass any standardised test that's around. We can do all that by providing very small classes and having added extras, like going to Hunter College once a week to attend science lectures to complement the school's curricular work.

In addition we offer tutorials – at seven in the morning, at lunchtimes, after school, sometimes until seven in the evening. Some are one to one, others are in small groups, all are part of our extensive extra-curricular programme. Another aspect of creating a normal school environment is that we offer a full range of extra-curricular activities, which is unusual for alternative high schools. Along with basketball and other sports, we have a debating club, just as you'd find in any mainstream high school. Our club entered a city wide debate competition and made it into the top eight of 205 schools in New York City – not once, but twice. We want them to be involved in multiculturalism, in internationalism, in everything that takes them beyond the walls of the Bronx.

Taking its place in the community

Bringing parents on board is a priority for a school serving a population where parents themselves may have no experience of high school. Special Saturday classes are run for parents in English as a second language, computers, arts and crafts and general education diplomas in Spanish and English; there are also counsellors on site with whom parents can talk about drug prevention, domestic violence or how to support their children's studies. It's a measure of their success that they regularly get seventy or so parents in on a Saturday. In Dr Cataldi's words, 'Our school is like a village that's raising not only the child but the parent, too'.

Another way of helping both parents and children is to keep the school open virtually year-round, including over the Christmas, Easter and summer holidays. When there's nowhere for them to go, when home is a place lacking in food and warmth, when parents are frightened for them to be out, the natural answer is to have them come into school, where they know they're safe, fed, looked after and engaged in activities that are intellectually and physically healthy. 'Our school's really a home from home for some of our students, and for a few, it's their primary home,' says Cataldi.

Staff, some of them Hispanic themselves, understand, accept and appear to be non-judgmental about the fact that for a multitude of reasons – socio-economic, political, personal – many parents have not been able to give these children the basic skills and sense of stability and the aspirations that they need to fulfill their potential. 'We believe that the missing component in our students' lives is a sense of security and nurturing,' says Vicky, and continues:

So what we present them with is a safe environment but one that makes demands on them that they invariably respond to, using a curriculum that has been raised to the standard of some of the stiffest curricula of some of the most prestigious schools – public and private – in New York City. And it works. We see that any student can make it with the right types of nurturing and assistance. What we're doing is providing these students, the majority of them young women, with a chance to achieve higher than they would in mainstream, where they're turned off by teachers and by young men. And we're also giving them high expectations, so that they're steered into career choices that will give them a more positive future.

High flying kids in low income neighbourhoods

High standards are central to the school's philosophy and ethos. The logistics of the school help. Being accommodated within Hostos Community College allows HLA students to take college courses once they have achieved a good level in the subject within the high school curriculum. At the moment, forty students are attending college courses, taking everything from calculus to psychology, English literature to languages. Not only does this put them into the higher powered college world with higher powered role models all around them, but it means that college credits can be taken while still at high school, thereby cutting down the time – expensive time – they'll need to be spending at college once they graduate from high school. It makes going to college seem normal, a natural progression from high school. And, as Cataldi says, 'it's vital that they experience success and once they do, success in one subject breeds success in others.' There is also an advanced placement history course for fast trackers and an honour roll for the top students, both innovations in the genre of alternative schools where sights are often set much lower.

High career aspirations are part of the picture, too. The school arranges internships (work experience placements) that reflect students' interests and their dreams. Some seniors (18 year olds) with artistic talents have had placements at the Metropolitan Museum of Art. If you were to translate this to a British equivalent, it would be like sending young people from a pupil referral unit to the Tate Gallery for two weeks. The school also has an arrangement with some local hospitals to give students part-time summer jobs as medical assistants, for which they're trained. The idea is that they have an alternative to working in a no-hope fast food joint when they graduate and have to work their way through college; it's also that they get to know career options in the medical and para-medical world.

The day I spent talking to staff and students, an Asian girl who was particularly keen on science was asked by Dr Cataldi what career she was thinking of entering. When she said she wanted to be a nurse, he pulled her up short. 'Why a nurse? Why not a doctor?' Then she pulled him up short. 'Because I like science but I'm not so good at math.' Undeterred, the irrepressible principal managed to have the last word. 'Then you need to be going to after school tutorials in math, don't you, so you can choose to be a doctor. See Mrs So-and-So after class.'

His style may be heavy-handed but it's altogether in character for a man who arrived in New York City in the late 1950s as a teenage immigrant himself, not speaking a word of English. He didn't manage to get a 'proper' academic high school diploma back then, just scraping by with a GED, the general education diploma designed for unacademic low achievers who then carry the stigma of being second rate around with them forevermore. But Cataldi managed to throw the impediment off in due course and today has a PhD in comparative literature. He sees his greatest achievement, though, as running an alternative high school that is offering success to those who have never experienced it before and whose excellence has brought it national and international coverage and interest from the pages of *Newsweek* to French television and German magazines.

He could earn more money in a better resourced school district but, he says as tears begin to flood his eyes:

These kids, they remind me of the way I was when I first came here. I have a lot in commmon with them in terms of culture, background and experience. I tell them about how it was for me back then and they see me as a role model. But the truth is that kids today need more than what they needed 30 and 40 years ago. Today, we're having to change a mentality, an attitude.

Running HLAS is a constant juggling act. Despite the fact that the school takes in young people suspended from other schools, some with emotional and behaviour difficulties, the city's board of education doesn't allocate enough resources, in the principal's view.

'It costs $8,330 a year to educate a child in New York City,' says Dr Cataldi. 'But here, we get $7,033. Because we get a grant from the State of $800 per student to hire more teachers and for our after school programmes, the City thinks we don't need more. Compare either of those figures to the $21,000 Westchester County (a rich suburb neighbouring New York City) was spending per year per child.

Then there's the problem of getting teachers. Given the extraordinarily long, extra unpaid hours during which they tutor and counsel as well as run sports and other activities, it's no wonder. But a problem even more fundamental is luring teachers to the deeply unsalubrious Mott Haven area in which the school is located, where the tip of the South Bronx meets the northern part of Manhattan, which incorporates a section of Harlem. Staff turnover is high. Newly qualified teachers come for two or three years and then move on to other better areas where they receive higher salaries because of the experience they've gained working in this tough neighbourhood. 'We're a training ground for suburban schools,' is how Cataldi sees it.

Not a job, rather a calling

But bitterness doesn't seem to be part of his emotional make-up. Like the Hollywood representations of teachers in 'Dangerous Minds,' 'To Sir with Love,' and 'The Blackboard Jungle,' Cataldi and his senior staff, who have been at the school since the beginning, don't have jobs so much as vocations. Only with that kind of body and soul attitude could they work, day in day out, year in year out, lavishing the amount of time and energy they do on getting their students on track, keeping them in one piece and making sure they're catapulted over the ghetto wall.

When you consider that 65% of Hispanic students in New York City never graduate and when you take into account the different levels of impoverishment in which these young people live in what can only be described as a third world environment within the richest country in the world, what is taking place behind the rickety doors of Hostos Lincoln Academy of Science is nothing short of a miracle. It's not 'alternative' in the radical 60s and 70s sense, it may not emphasise creative expression or freedom of the individual to choose a syllabus most suited to their interests, but it's certainly an alternative to what other kids identified as potential drop-outs are getting: the experience of success and the motivation to continue their education, wherever that may take them.

Snapshots of Hostos Lincoln students

Martine, aged 16, came to New York from Venezuela six years ago :

When I finished junior high school, one of the teachers advised my mother to send me to Hostos. At junior high, I was considered a bad student because my behaviour was bad. There, all they did was teach me English. I didn't learn anything else about this country and the way things work and it was a waste of time. It was the right choice for me to come here. Because it's a small school, teachers are always on top of you. If you do something bad, they call your mother. They wouldn't do this in a bigger school. That's what's made me improve. Hostos has also helped me learn about the government and social issues in the USA and about how everything's broken down. Now I'm doing really good and getting high scores.

Erma 16, is a Kosovan refugee who has been in the United States for two years:

I transferred from another high school after being there for a half a year. There, my grades were going down all the time. Teachers weren't after you to find out how you were doing. If you just do the work and come to class, that's all they want to know. They don't really worry about you. At Hostos Lincoln, teachers want to know how you're doing all the time and make sure you're learning. Until you learn what you're supposed to, they won't let you go. And security guards here make sure students don't cut classes. Not just that, but when everybody knows each other in a small school like this, students will tell teachers if they see you cutting.

Manuel, a Hispanic boy, is a former student. Dr. Cataldi tells his story.

Manuel came from another high school after he'd been suspended. He was one of those boys that most teachers would've washed their hands of. When he came for his interview, I asked him what he wanted to do with his life. He said he wanted to be a doctor. I was surprised until he told me his story. He'd been stabbed in the street by another youth and had his life saved by a trauma surgeon. That experience seems to have changed his whole attitude. He applied himself well here, doing chemistry and cellular biology while studying radiology at a local hospital and now is in his third year at the University of Georgia. Who knows? Maybe one day he'll save my life.

Gil, of Puerto Rican descent, is another former student. His story is told by assistant principal Nicholas Mazzarella:

Gil was referred to Hostos Lincoln Academy by his middle school counselor because he was at high risk of dropping out if he were to go to a large high school. He came from a very poor single parent family living in a high crime neighbourhood where he was a particular target of bullies. Since the age of ten, he had suffered from alopecia and had been constantly tormented for being bald. His reaction was to become anti-social. When he came to our summer programme before entering ninth grade, we saw that he had excellent computer and art skills. So the staff used those skills as a tool to get him involved with other students. He became a peer tutor to others and as a result, developed a circle of friends. While he had failed some of his subjects at middle school, here he started to pass all his classes and began to excel academically. HLAS got him a part-time job at the Bronx Museum of Art in the graphic art department, where he became an expert in computer graphic arts. At school, he became involved in a lot of activities and graduated in the normal time. He went on to Buffalo University and is now working for a computer company and finishing a Masters degree. He's married with one child. And he's still bald.

Jefferson County High School, Louisville, Kentucky
An example of constructive deconstruction

Jefferson County High is a school based on a simple if ingenious concept. If conventional schools are not accessible to young people leading unconventional lives or to those who can't or won't conform to school schedules and regimes, the solution is to create a school that breaks conventions of structure and scheduling and makes itself available to people with complex needs. In this restructured school, students take responsiblity for setting their own pace and work only on what they need in order to graduate. While this may sound not dissimilar from further education colleges in the UK, there is a crucial difference: at Jefferson County, there are no taught classes. Everyone works on their own individualised study programmes, using computer-assisted instruction programmes that take them through their course of studies, step by step, at the pace the student chooses. All work is done at school and under the supervision of teachers who are there to pass them on to the next stage and help them when they need it.

Designed by two veteran adult educationalists, Buell Snyder and Beverley Herrlinger, the aim was to create a school that would offer young people the same flexible options for achieving their high school diplomas as adults had in night schools or correspondence courses; a school that would fit into young people's lives rather than forcing the young people to fit into the school and would allow them to work independently but with the advantage of having help on hand when they needed it. Acknowledging the fact that the vast majority of local students have jobs, some of them full-time, and that it was difficult if not impossible to attend school six hours a day, do homework and work at their jobs, they devised a model that drew on the flexibility and shortened hours of adult education.

The doors to Snyder and Herrlinger's revolutionary high school were opened 13 years ago in Louisville, Kentucky. Originally based on one site, the school district was so impressed with the concept and with the clamour for places once people got wind of it that they asked for replicas to be set up in four other sites scattered around the city.

Acknowledging the reality of students' lives

The reason for the popularity is in large part down to its flexibility. This is a school that students attend in three hour blocks. There are sessions running in the morning, in the afternoon and in the evening and students are free to fit sessions into their day as they see fit. The idea is that three hours give sufficient time to accomplish a substantial amount of work without being so long a stretch that it leads to frustration and boredom. Students set their own schedules, based on what credits they need to graduate, and their own pace, depending on what other commitments they have. Teenage mothers with childcare arrangements to fit around or young people who have jobs or who look after sick or elderly relatives might only come for the minimum three hours a day a few times a week. Most students come for a single block. Those with more leeway or who are in a particular hurry can come for more. Open entry means that anyone can join at any time, starting at whatever level is appropriate to them and working on their individualised curriculum at their own pace. Most days, at least one new student comes on board. And it's all free, run by the Jefferson County Board of Education.

The range of students that are either referred by their previous schools or self-refer is impressive. Some are children of school board members, state legislators, local media personalities. Some are at the opposite end of the socio-economic spectrum. A few live in cars. A very small number have been through the youth justice system. A large majority –

80% – are young parents. Most, between 70 and 80%, work, many of them in full time jobs. Academically, they tend not to be low achievers but, in Beverley's words, 'they're kids who sit at the back of the room, put their heads down and drop out in their minds. They're generally good old average kids – not gifted, not slow.' A very small proportion are high-achieving.

Jefferson County High is, in the view of Jay Smink, director of the National Dropout Prevention Center 'a unique concept, ahead of all the others'. Its special blend of individualised learning, flexible hours and support on demand has proven to be wildly popular with students in the area and with educationalists far beyond the city limits of Louisville. The Jefferson County curriculum model has been taken up by and replicated in 250 school districts in twenty three states across America. 'I don't know how they hear about us, but people from all over the country write in or come to visit our school,' says Beverley Herrlinger, whose position as coordinator of the school puts her in charge of staff training and curriculum development.

In Louisville, over 5,000 students have graduated from JCHS since the school opened in 1986, averaging 450 graduates a year. The staying on rate is around 72%. Compared to the school district retention rate of 95%, it doesn't look that good. But the dropout rate reflects the fact that the student population being served is the most at risk in the area. What the figures don't show is that more than half those who dropout come back and graduate later, sometimes after a year or two when they feel they're ready to see things through. 'If they drop out, we tell them 'we'll be here for you when you come back,' says Beverley Herrlinger. There aren't many schools that will say that.

A particular formula for a particular kind of student

Buell Snyder, who is principal of Jefferson County, explains how he and Herrlinger came to create a new curriculum that had never been tried before:

> Saying that this is the answer for all kids is the same as saying that regular school is the answer for all kids. This is an option, offering a different teaching style for those who need it. It's for a specific kind of student who prefers working on their own at their own pace. When we started designing it, there was nowhere else con-

centrating on academic study for ordinary kids who were dropping out. When we looked at who the drop-outs were, we found that they weren't troublemakers but regular students who didn't fit in. Those were the students we wanted to attract.

This is how Jefferson County works. When students first enter the school, they undergo a diagnostic assessment based on standardised achievement tests to determine their strengths and weaknesses in literacy and numeracy. From the data provided by this assessment, instructors plan for each student an individual basic skills programme. Those who test low on maths but high on English, for example, would be required to go through a study programme that focused on bringing them up to a set level in maths. The assessment also determines at what stage students can begin work on their individual programme of high school credited units. Once they reach a certain level they are permitted to begin a dual track programme of basic skills and unit work until they reach a high level of basic skills attainment, at which point they can drop it and concentrate on working towards their credits.

Studying takes place in a classroom with one qualified teacher and one instructor (non-qualified but who has a degree), rather like a well resourced small school. But there the resemblance with other schools ends. Each student is in an intense relationship with their individualised instruction plan, designed by the teacher and drawing on up to twenty commercially prepared books as well as twenty three computer assisted instruction (CAI) programmes. Snyder explains the thinking behind using CAIs.

> This gives students the flexibility they need. Not only is their progress monitored at each step, but it's responded to. They must correctly answer several questions in a row to be able to proceed to the next stage. If they don't, it holds them back until they manage to answer them correctly. It's designed to keep the problems challenging but not frustrating.

Teachers are kept updated on students' work by way of print-outs which specify where the problems are arising and indicate to them when and how to intervene. Since all the information is computerised and stored, if a student drops out for awhile, they can pick up where they left off when they eventually return.[1]

The beauty of the JCHS system is that the committed student won't fail, because the school won't allow them to. One particularly clever fail-safe device built into the programme is the way homework is organised. At ordinary school, it's left to the individual to go home, do the work and bring it in for grading. If you don't do it, you get marked down or have double work to do for the next lesson. That's fine for students with the organisational skills, motivation and the physical and mental space that homework requires. But it's anathema for those who don't. Realising this, homework at JCHS is transformed into school-work: it's done during class time. There are never assignments that must be completed out of class hours. So for someone like Mikeal, who has profound difficulties with carrying out assignments away from school, the problem is solved, as it is for students with children and those with demanding work schedules who would find it hard if not impossible to make the time at home. When all your work takes place at school, you never fall behind because you're working on your own and you set your own pace – even if you have to take a few days off because your child has measles.

The teacher as guide on the side

Needless to say, Jefferson County High is a very different work environment for teachers. Because of the unconventional role that teachers are required to assume, as well as the myriad problems that their students have and the close interaction between teachers and pupils, Herrlinger has devised a twelve hour pre-service training programme that all teachers must complete. Just as Jefferson County High isn't suitable for the student who is a team player and thrives on discussion, competition and cross-fertilisation of ideas, the kind of work required by teachers won't be everyone's cup of tea. 'Here, we don't have the teacher as sage on the stage, but rather as the guide on the side,' quips Herrlinger.

So rather than being teachers in the usual sense, staff serve as mentors as well as academic guides. A system like this couldn't exist otherwise. These are students who have suffered body blows to their self-esteem and have felt alienated from their peers and diminished as a result of their failure to stay on track. Switching off is one of the danger signals that teachers are trained to recognise the signs of. Herrlinger explains:

Most of the time, when students withdraw in regular school it's because they don't want to be called on in class. At our school, if they withdraw they aren't allowed to proceed to the next stage. We tell them upfront that their progress is up to them and that here, they're given responsibility for their own fate. They can't just slide by. We won't permit them to.

The way cognitive difficulties are dealt with is different, too. If a student is doing work and keeps getting the wrong answer, causing them to go over and over the same part of the programme, it's in private. Nobody is pressurising them to hurry up. Says Herrlinger:

> Some students work very quickly, others very slowly. We take pains to get them to understand that it's not time that's important with us, it's performance. With the CAI work, students get help from one of the two teachers in the classrom if they get stuck. They have to do every assignment and hand it in. The teacher grades it and if she or he passes it, the student is allowed to go on. If they don't pass it, the student's required to complete the assignment again. This way, the student builds on success, not failure.

The staff at JCHS are all too aware of the fact that for many of their students, coming in to school for whatever length of time they choose to is a supreme effort. (Although three hours is the norm, a minority come for three hours in the morning and then return in the evening for another block.) It means confronting their failures and working hard to overcome them. So as well as there being a counsellor at each of the five sites from which the school operates, every teacher is a counsellor in their own right. In the words of Dr Buddy Revells, a former Baptist minister and now a teacher at JCHS:

> Every teacher sees part of their job as responding to the needs of the disaffected children they're dealing with in a warm, caring, loving way. One of the things that all the young people here have in common is the need for someone to call them by their name, to give them the feeling that someone stands with them, affirms them and accepts them.

Parents as partners

But the school also recognises its limitations. 'Parents are the most important variable in this equation' says Revells, 'Without their love, care and support, schools can only put a band-aid on the hurt that these young people suffer.' What is certain is that when a child is failing to attend school or is being disruptive in class and is getting negative feedback from their mainstream schools, parents themselves suffer enormous stress and often find it difficult to support their children – or even to like them sometimes. Whether they are the cause of their children's behaviour or merely appalled witnesses to it, it's important, as far as Jefferson County High School is concerned, to make connections with them.

For this reason, Dr Revells runs what he calls a parents' recovery group each semester to get them to offload their problems and work out how to deal with them.

> We spend a couple of hours talking about who their teenager is at this age. We try to develop strategies for dealing with them and then share with each other not just information but comfort and stability. One of the things we attempt to do is normalise the feelings that parents have towards their children. Usually they're frustrated, angry, bewildered and astonished at what their children are doing. In these workshops we say 'it's okay to feel that way but here's some ideas for taking that energy and transposing it into something healthy and creative for both of you."

The success of JCHS's approach is reflected in the school's statistics. Approximately 2,500 recent drop-outs (under the age of 21) come to JCHS every year to pursue their education. In addition, around 325 adults (over 21) attend. Altogether, 400 students receive their high school diplomas from the school each year. While everyone enters and finishes their studies at different times (the average completion time is eighteen months), the school puts a lot of effort into acknowledging students' achievements with two high school graduation ceremonies every year, with students taking part in one or the other according to when they've completed their studies. The ceremonies are just like mainstream schools', where students receive their diplomas in cap and gown and a top student gives a formal speech to an audience of family and friends.

Beverley Herrlinger remembers a particular poignant ceremony:

There was one young woman who came to us when the school had only recently opened. She'd been kicked out of another alternative high school for children with severe discipline problems. And she certainly had them. She'd attempted suicide, been pregnant three or four times and had shot her ex-boyfriend. When we discovered her background, staff said 'there's no way we're going to be successful with her.' But she proved us wrong. She completed all the credits she needed and ended up giving the formal speech at the graduation ceremony, in which she said that our school had changed her life because for the first time, she was accepted for who she was.

Another unlikely success story is recalled by principal Buell Snyder:

There have been a lot of students who've come here over the years who we've thought we wouldn't be able to do anything with. But there was one in particular that stands out for me. He was 17 years old with long hair, piercings all over his face, tattered jeans and long chains on his clothes and wrists. His behaviour caused quite a bit of havoc when he first came and I thought I'd have to remove him from the school. But he convinced me to give him another chance and over the next eighteen months he applied himself and graduated, although always remaining the non-conformist. At the graduation ceremony, his name was called to receive his diploma, but no one recognised him when he walked across the stage. Here was this clean-shaven young man, wearing a suit and tie with his hair neatly cut. There were tears in both our eyes as he grabbed my hand and thanked me for giving him another chance. He's in college now.

You're never too old at Jefferson County

What their experiences in setting up and running Jefferson County High School have shown Buell and Beverley is that disaffection is no respecter of gender, race, class or age. Nor era. Throughout this century and many more before, there have been children who have felt unable to cope with being forced into the institutional life of schools, no matter how big or small the size of the school, no matter how clever or slow they were. Or there were other reasons why they couldn't go to school. One of the memorable cases was that of a woman who came to Jefferson County High at the age of 65. Beverley tells the story:

She had lived on a farm as a young girl in a rural part of Kentucky and went to a one room schoolhouse. Every morning the young boy who lived in the farmhouse next door would pick her up and they would walk together to school. And every afternoon, they'd walk home together.

One day her teacher said to her 'you know, if you continue walking back and forth with that young man, people gonna talk about you'. Well, being a very proper young lady, rather than have the neighbours talk about her, she quit school. And she didn't return until she came to Jefferson County at the age of 65. For three years, she worked through all the credits she needed, sitting amongst fellow students who were the age of her grandchildren.

A few years later, the assistant principal of our school read in the newspaper that she'd passed away. He went down to the funeral home to pay his respects and when he came back, his eyes were full of tears and he could barely speak. After he became composed, he told us that the woman's son had come up to him and told him how happy he was to see him there and invited him to come and view the casket. When they went over, our assistant principal looked down and saw that lying right beside the lady was her high school diploma. She had asked to be buried with it because it had meant so much to her. She had achieved her goal after a lifetime.

Conclusion

Hostos Lincoln and Jefferson County are two very different schools offering their own unique ways of motivating students and ensuring that they succeed. While distinct from each other, they share certain important elements.

Both fly in the face of contemporary alternative education approaches. At both schools, expectations and standards are high. Students follow the curriculum taught to all mainstream students and teachers expect them to see it through. Whatever happened in their past to lead them to seek alternative education is put behind them in the school's eyes. They're not seen as problems but as individuals pursuing their studies.

How these schools assume these approaches and, just as importantly, encourage these erstwhile disaffected youth to go on to fulfill their potential is all a question of attitude. Size helps, too, but it doesn't explain why smaller alternative high schools around the United States aren't distinguishing themselves academically. What appears to underpin the attitudes of staff of both these schools is the belief in their students' power to overcome their difficulties with the right level of support. Support comes in all shapes and guises. When you're dealing with young people who have a history of conflict with teachers and schools, they are likely to be hypersensitive to the way teachers interact with them. The minute they sense a patronising turn of phrase or, conversely, a lack of understanding, that familiar slippery slope is ready and waiting for them.

There's one word that I have heard time and again from students at these schools and at others that are endeavouring to create new, positive environments. It's respect. Trite, perhaps, but it says volumes about what young people crave and are not getting in big, impersonal schools that see the masses rather than the individuals and look at all but the achievers as problems rather than as young people requiring attention.

Is it idealistic, naive or just plain daft to talk of respectfulness towards students, some of whom may be exhibiting difficult behaviour? If it is, then we can all tear up the government's directives on lowering exclusion rates and denounce social inclusion as unattainable codswollop, pie in the sky devised by politicians who don't know one end of a classroom from another. And we can look forward to many more generations of young people who fall off the edge – or are pushed over it.

If we are going to listen to children and young people and, in doing so, attempt to prioritise respectfulness towards them as essential a component of education reform as the curriculum and assessment, then it needs to be done within a holistic framework. We need to take into account staff and also scheduling, class size, availability of tutorials, the way feedback is delivered and sanctions. As Kathleen Lynch and Anne Lodge of University College, Dublin put it:

> Young people are being socialised into conformity and obedience. How valuable such a cultural climate is for the development of responsibility and initiative is an open question...

Granting equality of respect demands changes in the organisational practices of many of our public institutions; most conspicuously, it requires a greater democratisation of schooling for all age groups, and of other health and welfare services which care for children (K. Lynch and Anne Lodge, 'Power as an Equality Issue in Schools – a Question of Lack of Respect', paper presented at BERA, 1998).

What Hostos Lincoln and Jefferson County High illustrate above all is a respect for the troubled young people they serve, a belief in their powers to transcend their past and present problems and a commitment to help them reclaim their futures.

Profiles of three very different students attending Jefferson County High School for very different reasons

LISA

Lisa is a white, middle class 19 year old. Last year, she was on the honour roll at the most prestigious high school in Louisville. As well as being bright and articulate, she was popular and active in the life of the school community. She'd been on her junior and senior high school dance teams (similar to cheerleaders) for seven years, always a barometer of all-American wholesomeness. She had everything going for her and was looking forward to a bright future at university.

Then last year, in her final year, she went off the rails.

> I decided I didn't like school anymore. I'd stay away from classes, sleeping or walking around the mall on my own. I wasn't drinking or taking drugs, but I got depressed and didn't get on with my parents. My parents had divorced a few years before and then my stepdad had died. The counselor I went to suggested that everything had built up. I don't know, but whatever the reasons, I got myself into a mess. I moved out and got an apartment on my own and got a job and hated my whole life. I was so lonely. I didn't even see my friends very much. Except when I went to my class' high school graduation and sat in the stands by myself and I saw all my friends down there getting their diplomas and couldn't believe that I wasn't down there, too and I just cried and cried.

After about four months of not talking to my family or anybody, I was hungry and lonely and went to my mom's and said I wanted to come home. I still had to work to pay off my debts but in the evenings, I'd read all the classics I could lay my hands on. I told my mom I had to go back to school to use my mind. My counselor told me about Jefferson County and said that I could get the credits I needed to graduate there.

When I interviewed Lisa, she'd been at Jefferson County High School for a month and was on course to graduate, having earned all the English credits she needed, within four weeks. She was unrecognisable from the person she'd described.

At my previous high school, we all learned everything as a class together. The big difference is that here, it's all individualised help. There's no taught lessons. You go to a teacher for help and you know that they're rooting for you. I'm moving quickly through the coursework I need to do in order to take my exams, faster than I could've done in school because I'm only studying for the English credits I need three hours a day, five days a week instead of one forty five minute session a week that I'd be doing in my previous school. For the time I'm here, I'm totally focused on the work. I don't talk to anybody, I don't even know anybody and I don't care what clothes I put on. I'm just here to do the work.

The postscript is that Lisa went on to complete her studies within the month and is now applying to universities. She wants to major in political science and hopes to go on to law school. Her mother is 'beside herself with happiness'.

Kids like white, middle class Lisa aren't too thick on the ground in the South Bronx. But the experiences that knocked her resiliency out of whack and plunged her into a mire of alienating depression will be familiar to young people whether in the ghetto, in the suburbs, in the USA, Britain or anywhere else. So, too, will the experiences of Michael and Mikeal.

MICHAEL is a 20 year old African American

It's been a rocky road for me. When I was very young, I was abused by my mother's boyfriends. Then with my stepfather, it was more mental abuse. We never got on. Both my mother and stepfather were university graduates, but there was an unwritten taboo in my house that one who speaks freely will do other things freely too. Their biggest fear was that me and my sister would disobey and speak against them. Because my ideas were never listened to, I locked them away as a defense mechanism When I wanted to retrieve them, I couldn't get them because I was so used to holding myself back.

At school, things were difficult, too. At my previous high school, I was bullied because I was an easy target: small and brainy. I couldn't fit in with the majority because I was different. People like me who like books and constantly use what they learn in books are seen as nerds and show-offs. I wasn't a show-off. I can't help speaking articulately the way I do. I've spoken like this since I was four.

Academically, some of my teachers couldn't understand me because I had difficulty with writing. I could talk up a storm but was phobic about pencils and papers. I was afraid of airing my views and also about formulating ideas. Because of my writing problems, I was held back in tenth grade two years in a row. Why they gave me the same teacher both years, I'll never know. Obviously I had a problem with the curriculum and how it was being taught. I kind of lost hope and the second time around, I left after a semester because I felt I wasn't getting anywhere. I'd gotten two credits for the whole time I was in high school: to graduate, I needed twenty. Being held back twice degrades you. When everyone in your class passes you by and they're seniors (in twelfth grade) and you're still in tenth grade, there's something really wrong. Being 20 years old and in eleventh grade (when students are 17) isn't someting to be proud of.

Because of the situation at home, I moved out when I was 18. It was for my survival. Rather than living in constant conflict, I decided it was better to live on my own. I first came to Jefferson County High School last year and stayed for two months but because I had to work to pay my bills, I left and came back eight months later. I've been here now two months. According to my graduation plan, the level I'm working at now is equivalent to eleventh grade. I'm going to continue coming six hours a day and hope to graduate in four or five months.

Since being here, my mind has become liberated. I get As for all my written work. I feel that my ideas are all there. It's like people waiting in line for the subway. Now I'm happy when asked to write a poem.

And I know that I have to graduate, for myself. With a piece of paper saying what I've achieved, I'd no longer be the educational fool who knew everything and had nothing to show for it.

MIKEAL, 19, African American

Basically I'm not a bad kid but I just don't like homework. It was my biggest problem at my previous school. I was never in trouble there except for not wanting to do homework. I just thought it was unnecessary. When I did do it, I'd try to get it over with as quickly as possible. It used to drive my parents crazy. I mostly got Cs, Ds and Fs but I liked English, band and gym. Some of my friends were bad and others were straight A kids. When my parents said they wanted me to come to Jefferson County, I thought it would be full of bad kids and I didn't know if I wanted to come. But when I came, I saw that instead of disorder, it was orderly and quiet. And when they told me the format, that you work at your own pace, I decided I liked it. I come usually three or four hours a day and do history, anatomy and geometry. My grades are excellent. And there's no homework to do here, because you do it all while you're here. I'm pushing myself more here than I did in my old school, when I was on their schedule which told you 'take the test today, do the homework tomorrow'. I'm much better at pacing myself and I move more quickly than if I had to fit in with everybody else.

References
1.   Gross, B. 'Phi Delta Kappan', April, 1990.

CHAPTER SEVEN

HELPING SCHOOLS HELP THEIR STUDENTS: TWO PROGRAMMES

A blame culture has built up around schools over the last few decades. Youth crime, teen pregnancies, behaviour disorders, truancy, exclusion and drop-out rates are all on the rise. And since school is the common denominator of all children's lives, the thinking goes, schools must be the source of the social ills that our children contract, like a virus sweeping through the classrooms of the nation. They are vilified for being too liberal, failing to draw clear boundaries for children and not equipping them with the knowledge base they need for the future. Or they are castigated for being too regimented, not allowing children to express themselves and to be seen as individuals, leading them into anti-social behaviour out of frustration and boredom. While there are some grounds for both positions, to lay all social problems at schools' collective feet is mistaken, unfair and counter-productive. No school is an island unto itself.

Children live in the world, not at school. Their home environment, popular culture and their community have more influence on their lives than schools could ever aspire to. They come into school with experiences that are diverse and often unfathomable. We all know in theory how profound an impact poverty and the myriad effects of social deprivation can have on the emotional, behavioural and academic experiences of children. But do we really understand what it does to a child to suffer physical or emotional violence or the threat of it day after day or to have to sleep in shifts with siblings because there aren't enough beds or to have to lie to cover up the truth of why their mum never comes up to school?

No matter what their social, economic or ethnic background, no child in the world has ever come into school with a clean slate; there is always baggage, whether it's good, bad or somewhere in between. It's the resiliency of the child, in the end, that is the most decisive factor in their fate. And that is something that educationalists can to some degree help with.

Schools can have an enormous impact on children's self-esteem and on their social and academic progress. But for at-risk young people going home to abuse or apathy, to criticism or neediness, school can only do so much. There is growing awareness that a buffer zone between school and home can do much to bolster the young people in the fight against disaffection.

In the UK, in other countries in the European Union, in Australia and in the United States, multi-agency support is more and more being seen as the answer. Where schools are hard-pressed to meet even the academic needs of their diverse populations, attempting to meet their other pressing needs is overwhelming. But the concept of using schools as the base from which to bring in other agencies – social services, health and mental health services – is one that makes sense in the new era of joined up thinking that New Labour has spearheaded. A coordinated approach to delivering services for children, such as the model pioneered in Manchester under the banner of Children's Services, is a giant step forward. The government's Youth Support Services intends, once up and running, to eradicate the disjointed, fragmentary way that services have been planned and delivered up until now.

Before we look at two multi-agency programmes in the United States that work with schools to target disaffected students in new and in-spired ways, I want to briefly describe an outstanding example of a particularly holistic, community-based approach instigated by the headteacher of a primary school in Newcastle in England. It is an object lesson in what is possible.

Culture of hopelessness on Tyneside

The east end of Newcastle is as desolate an example of social blight as you're likely to see on either side of the Atlantic. Unlike the South Bronx, there's no hustle and bustle. Here, it's just the odd shuffle you see of women every now and then ducking out to the corner shop.

Situated on the riverfront, this is a neighbourhood that once resonated to the thunder of 12,000 men trooping off to work at the naval ship-yards every morning. It was in the early 1980s that the thunder was silenced, as the shipyards closed and the troops were forced to hang up their workboots. For almost all of them, it was forever.

When Norma Redfearn took over the headship of West Walker Primary School in 1986, the hopelessness hung in the air like thick black smoke. Herself the daughter of a former shipyard worker, she found a community in which the men's pain and despair had wafted through the very fabric of the community, infecting wives and children, too.

> My feeling when I came here was that here were parents who had nothing to look forward to in their lives. I wanted to raise the standards of children's learning but it seemed to me that the community didn't value the learning process. Education hadn't benefited them, and their attitude to the school was very negative. Children would say to me 'what's the point of learning when there's no jobs, me ma says'. I realised that I had to work with the parents if I was to change the attitudes of the children so that they could begin to learn.

You didn't have to look too hard to see that these children, nearly three quarters of whom were on free school meals, weren't learning. Twenty per cent of children didn't show up to school at all; of those who did attend, many would roll in an hour or more late and some would bunk for part of the day. 'When I first came, I'd have to stand out on the streets looking for children who'd run away from school,' says Red-fearn. Unsurprisingly, SATs results were well below the national average; children were leaving Year 6 to start secondary school unable to read and do maths.

The headteacher as civic entrepreneur

Redfearn decided that to make an impact, she was going to have to work on a number of different fronts simultaneously with both parents and children. 'I wanted to give the children and their parents some inner pride, some dignity. I knew that there was tremendous talent and skill among them, but I needed to work with outside agencies to bring it out and maximise it. I couldn't do it on my own.'

Despite the initial suspicions of the local community and resistance by the local authority to regarding education in quite so holistic a way, Redfearn set to work creating school-based projects that met the needs of the entire community. For children, she set up a breakfast club because she knew a large proportion of children were coming into school hungry and were unable to learn because of it. She developed literacy and numeracy projects – predating the national schemes – to get the children up to the appropriate levels. She arranged business partnership schemes to help get children into the work ethic of good timekeeping, honouring homework deadlines, etc. And she arranged mentoring schemes with workers in local industries 'to show them a world of work these kids and their parents have never known.' She inviegled a local group of architects into working with parents and children to create a playpark where there had once stood a tatty playground, too.

For the grown-ups, a community wing was set up in a disused part of the school which has become the home of the West Walker Community Association. The formally constituted group, formed as a result of Redfearn's drive to engage the community, has been at the forefront of planning services that local people felt they needed. The community wing houses a wide range of provision that comes under the title of Family Support, where multi-agency services offer advice, information and advocacy, one to one support and also interest groups for people with low self-esteem, adult education courses, crèche provision, a cafe, a computer room for IT training, a group for socially isolated women that focuses on assertiveness skills and confidence building, a group for parents of children with special needs, a men's group, and a young women's and girls' support group called Girlzone. There is also a community library. Thanks to Norma Redfearn's entrenpreneurial spirit, she was able to get funding from the local authority and health authority as well as from local businesses for all these innovations. Some things came easier than others. Last year, she won a ten year battle to get a full-time social services family support worker based at the school.

It was vital to base these services at the school, which is situated in a Social Priority Area, despite town hall bureaucrats' protestations that the locals should get on a bus like everyone else. She explains:

We're talking about a local community where people wouldn't cross the main road. It's important that things are offered here, in their own neighbourhood. Particularly with the support worker – families wouldn't go to see her at social services. It's like going to the police. Because she's here, she can help to prevent serious things from happening because people can see her straight away.

Plans are underway to expand the community wing to incorporate a Healthy Living Centre, which would provide healthcare services and advice.

It was a struggle all around to convince the local authority and others in the community of the wisdom in using the school as a community base as a way of boosting children's futures directly and indirectly. While enlightened educationalists around the world talk of school based multi-agency services as the way for the future and as the government declares the need for joined up collaborations between different sectors, it was Norma Redfearn's instincts that propelled her into taking action to achieve those very things:

I'm determined to give these children a sense of success so that they can go out feeling good when they start secondary school. The truth is there for all to see: the children running around in the streets in Newcastle and all over the country are children who have failed in primary schools.

Redfearn's commitment to her community has won her acclaim beyond the east end of Newcastle. She became the first headteacher to receive the prize for Public Management Leadership awarded by the Office for Public Management in 1997 and, the following year, was chosen by the think tank Demos as an example of civic entrepreneurship.

The following two examples of multi-agency collaborations in the United States brought about through voluntary sector initiatives are very different to Norma Redfearn's model but reflect the same holistic philosophy to learning: unless and until children's social and emotional needs are addressed, their potential is diminished. By working with schools that acknowledge that they can't be all things to all children and that they need outside assistance to deal with the complex and profound needs of their students, Communities in Schools and Teen

Outreach Programme are able to bring specialist expertise and support to thousands of at-risk children and young people all over the United States.

These two programmes represent very different approaches to the New Haven social development programme model because they target at risk students rather than working with the general student population. In addition, they draw on a range of strategies and support services. But they are yet another way of looking at how to improve children's academic chances by helping to improve their resilience.

Communities in Schools, Palm Beach County, Florida

Ask any American what they think of when you mention the name Palm Beach and it's certain to be palm trees, miles of sandy beaches and outrageous wealth as personified by Donald Trump and the Kennedy clan, both of whom have been Palm Beach homeowners.

It's a town that is known as the playground of the rich. Along with the well-heeled permanent residents, there are those who nip in and out of town for parties, weekend sunbathing and exclusive shopping trips. Some build houses the size of city blocks in hybrid styles that defy architectural description: Mexican baroque. Colonial ranch house. Disney Tudor. More numerous are what's known locally as the 'snowbirds'. They own condominiums overlooking the ocean and, as their name suggests, fly down to escape the icy winters of the east coast and midwest from March up until around June, when the Florida weather becomes as unbearable as what they have fled from, but at the opposite extreme of termperature. They are well-off and retired. And everyone knows that when you put wealth and age together, you get people who don't give a hang about the public school system – and don't mind who knows it.

Florida is a state in which there are no state taxes, because the would-be taxpayers have voted against them. They've voted against them because a large number of them are old and rich and don't need the public services that their taxes would support. Their children and grandchildren live thousands of miles to the north, they themselves have private health care and they don't mind paying tolls to drive on privately financed highways as smooth as butter. You have to try to understand something about these non-native, wealthy Floridians: these are people who have valet parking at their local supermarket.

Behind the palm-fringed facade

Now all this would be fine if everybody was as rich as these northerners and nobody needed public services. But nothing could be further from the truth. As well as being home to millionaires, the sprawling expanses of Palm Beach County contain some of the poorest people in the south. As well as white and black working poor and un-employed, there is a big, impoverished Hispanic population. How big is hard to say. Many are illegal and don't appear on any official statis-tical data: migrant workers who have come from Haiti, Honduras and Guatemala to the Sunshine State to work in the sugar cane industry and the citrus groves.

The huge economic divide, largely based on ethnicity, makes southern Florida look for all the world like South Africa. And nowhere is this more so than in its schools. While the state enjoys tremendous wealth thanks to citrus fruit, tourism and sugar cane, it ranks second from the bottom in the state by state national league tables for public school test scores. The rich send their children to private schools. As for the rest, they have all the problems you'd associate with poverty and depriva-tion, as well as difficulties peculiar to a transient, migrant community coming from the developing countries of Central America. The drop-out rate in Florida is around 25%; half of all Floridians fail to graduate through traditional routes, meaning that they either take GEDs (the lower level diploma for unacademic students) or they leave school and only get their diploma later, through night school or other adult educa-tion routes.

Against this perpetually sunny but deeply troubled backdrop, an organisation called Communities in Schools of Florida, Inc. has been working for the past 14 years to reverse the trend of disaffection and disenfranchisement in schools. It is affiliated to the national organisa-tion bearing the same name, a private, non-profit organisation that is the biggest dropout prevention programme in the United States. CIS originated in 1973 in Harlem originally under the name Cities and Schools and is committed to helping children to learn successfully, to stay in school and to prepare for life. It's predicated on four basic cornerstones. Every child needs and deserves:

- a safe place to learn and grow
- a marketable skill upon graduation
- a one to one relationship with a caring adult
- a chance to give back to community and peers

A matchmaking service to find the right answers to problems

A tall order, even for the big organisation that it is, with branches in thirty three states, including twelve county-wide programmes in Florida and reaching a total of more than 300,000 children – with another fifty four communities developing new programmes. CIS manages it by operating as a kind of matchmaking service, by linking appropriate community resources to school students at risk of dropping out. In Palm Beach County, it works with four voluntary organisations, putting them together with elementary, middle and high school students in twenty nine schools all over the county, including three alternative schools, amounting to over 30,000 children. Its initial aim in the county, to improve grades by 60% and attendance by 70%, has been surpassed in 14 years. The Palm Beach County school district has been so impressed with its ability to motivate and nurture students that it has adopted CIS as its dropout prevention programme.

Its methodologies are varied and dependent on the pupil population it's working with. There is classroom instruction, delivered by a CIS trained teacher based at the school who deals with issues like goal setting, problem solving and employability skills. There are student profile assessments, baseline assessments to identify children's strengths and weaknesses. There are peer mentoring and tutoring projects which are designed to help the mentor as much as the mentee. There are parenting workshops and CIS family outreach workers for families in crisis. There are also motivational guest speakers, job shadowing, counselling, youth leadership training, college scholarships and experiential learning trips.

Glades Community High School

One of the most innovative aspects of the programme is the Personal, Career and Social Development Skills course developed by CIS for elementary and high schools and taught by two team teachers. I spoke to one of the teachers and some of the students who attend the course at Glades Community High School.

To understand what the course is trying to achieve and under what circumstances, you need a snapshot of what the Glades district is like. An hour and a quarter's drive from Palm Beach, it could be a different country altogether – if not planet. The Glades is a rural area, as poor and featureless as Palm Beach is rich and glitzy. The two main industries are prisons and sugar cane, with a large Central American presence in both.

Most children in the area have experienced death at close hand. With the highest incidence of Aids in the state of Florida, it is not unheard of for parents to die and their children to find shelter in abandoned housing projects – and for drug dealers to prey on those kids. Housing for some is what you'd find in a developing country: wooden shacks with no running water, where children sleep in bunks in the kitchen. Some children can't come into school until the family receives their social security cheque so that they can buy shoes.

Such is the reputation of the place that when Glades High School students go on school outings to the theatre in Palm Beach, they are escorted by armed police. Self-esteem throughout the area is low, single parent families are the norm and the teen pregnancy rate is high. Last year, a girl with three children graduated from Glades. She came back to visit recently, pregnant with her fourth.

Giving students space, support and respect

Not a pretty picture. But what CIS is doing for these kids offers them hope and the building blocks to escape the dire circumstances in which they find themselves. Anne Haskell is CIS teacher and family outreach worker at the school, working with the Glades' most at-risk students. Unlike many teachers at the school, she's also a resident of Belle Glades, the down at heel main town of the area in which the school is located.

If community is the buffer zone between home and school, Anne is the buffer zone between the students and the school:

Working in school with the students and in their homes with their families, I'm able to understand why they're behaving the way they are at school and then relate that information to their other teachers to help them be a little more understanding. So if a child's sleeping in class or acting out, I'll talk to the teacher so they'll understand that he or she has been up since five in the morning doing domestic chores and looking after the younger ones. Then the teachers will hopefully feel they can work with the situation rather than just seeing it as a problem and moving quickly to get the student out of the classroom.

Anne Haskell and her team teaching colleague Greg Laws present a curriculum to troubled students that incorporates sex education, relationships, communication and negotiation skills and violence prevention. But that's only part of the picture. A lot of what's done is what she calls motivational work. She arranges for speakers from the community to talk about the work they do as law enforcement workers or at the Sheriff's drug farm (a labour camp type facility for adults who have been arrested for drug related offences). Sometimes she manages to bring inmates themselves in to talk to the students about how they came to be in their unenviable position and what it's like serving time. Others give talks on pregnancy prevention and birth control, suicide prevention and runaway services.

Defying preconceptions
Raising the expectations of young people who are surrounded by low expectations is a priority. 'Increasing self-esteem can make a big difference to those students staying in school and even going on to further education.' To this end, and to the disbelief of some, she arranges college tours for thirty of her students whom the rest of the world has written off.

I have the belief that if they can put their feet onto a college campus and visualise themselves there as students, they're more apt to feel it's a possiblity they can achieve. The hope is that they'll change the behaviours that keep them from getting the kinds of grades they need to get into college.

She also prioritises goal setting, something that is notoriously lacking in the lives of disaffected young people who are more often than not allowed to slide into failure:

The very first day of semester, I know who is coming so I have their report cards and I work out their grade point average [based on their current level of attainment. The highest grade point average is 4.0]. The students I have are almost all low achievers or need extra tutorial support because of a death in the family or other difficult circumstances. I say to them 'this is a reality check. This is where you are and you're here because your grades are low'. This past semester, something must have clicked. This grading period we've done better than ever before. I had one student with 4.0 and a few others with 3.75.

Team teaching in smaller classes is essential to the CIS ethos. Having two teachers in one room means that if and when there are crises – a death or illness in the family, a fight at school, a run-in with a teacher, abuse at home – the needy student can receive one to one attention while the other teacher takes over the class. The fact that it is a woman and a man teaching together is a felicitous bonus:

Very few of these kids have two adults at home. They see us as parent figures and as a male and female working together, communicating, agreeing, supporting each other, talking things over. Hopefully we're showiing what relationships can be like in a working context as well as personally.

What the class does is often led by what's happening at any given time. There was a period when Haskell concentrated on grief and loss because of the large number of recently bereaved children in the group. When I visited, the focus was on drugs because that was the biggest and most pressing problem at school.

As well as dealing with social and emotional issues, the CIS programme is there to get students the academic help they need by plugging them into the after school tutoring that the school runs. It's not as easy as it sounds. 'It can be a problem culturally,' says Anne Haskell, 'because parents want their kids at home after school where they can keep an eye on them. They're afraid that if they're not under their strict control, they'll get into trouble. So I go to the parents and explain why they're staying after school and get their permission to do the things that the kids want to do. We've had kids go on to college and have successful careers thanks to the programme and the tutoring that we've been able to get for them.'

One particularly surprising success story in recent years was revealed to Anne when she came back to school after being off sick for a couple of days. She found that the supply teacher taking her place had been one of her former CIS students who had had a child while still in high school and had lived through a difficult situation at home. But she overcame those difficulties, received a CIS scholarship to help towards college tuition costs (awarded to students who have proven their willingness to achieve), had gone to community college and went on to get her teaching degree.

One of her current students is Mesley Delba, an 18 year old Haitian who should be graduating this year but has been held back because of underachievement:

Being in CIS changed my life. I was skipping school and doing all wrong thing. But CIS teachers, they help me with a lot of thing. Sometime, when I have problem I talk to them and they help me solve that problem. If I need special help, they'll be there for me. I'll graduate next year if I do right thing this year. I want to go to college and do business studies.

Getting the young and at risk to believe in themselves by helping others

CIS also does early intervention work with academically floundering children in elementary and middle schools. At Boca Elementary School in Boca Raton, a suburb of Palm Beach with a substantial middle class population, a peer mentoring project in which at-risk fourth graders (11 year olds) 'teach' kindergartners (5 year olds) how to read is in operation. It's called the Buddy Programme and its effectiveness in raising self-esteem while at the same time enhancing literacy skills can be heard in what the CIS mentors themselves have to say about it.

Chris, an 11 year old boy: 'I like reading with little kids to make them read better. It also helps me. It makes me feel happier.'

Dorothy, also 11: 'It's helped my own reading a little bit. Sometimes when I read words in books I don't understand them. When I'm working with the little kids, that's when I get to know the words much better and get the hang of it.'

The children have all been referred by their third grade teachers, says Cynthia Boggs, CIS elementary school resource coordinator, because 'they all display signs of needing a safer place, a smaller class where they can get more attention than they receive at home. Some are here for academic problems, others for frequent absences or tardiness – all potential factors in dropping out later on. Once they're in a CIS class, we can provide more services for them than they would normally receive in mainstream.' The dozen or so children do all their subjects with the same teacher in the same classroom for two years, to give them a sense of security.

Their teacher, Patricia Norris, talks of the strong motivational strategies she employs as part of the CIS approach:

> This is all about trying to get them back on the right track before it's too late. One recent example I had shows how it can work. I had a girl who was virtually a non-reader at age nine. There were no behaviour problems, but she was very withdrawn and shy. She knew she couldn't read and felt defeated by it. I tried to find something she could do well and built up from there. I noticed that she was very good about sharing her things with others so I praised her a lot for that and it became her claim to fame. Then she started doing things for other people. Recently I arranged for her to be a helper in the office, running errands and doing odd jobs. Over the two years I've been working with her, her reading has improved dramatically. From a test score of zero she's now testing at 3.5, reading from a fifth grade reading book and volunteering to read in class when before, she would hide to avoid being called on.

It's not all down to what happens in the classroom. Ms Norris also 'pleaded' with the girl's grandmother, who she lives with, to read to her at home. Since then, grand daughter and granny have been reading together in the evenings.

Another motivating strategy is the quintessentially American sounding Earn Reading Bucks scheme. Children are encouraged to take home books with accompanying story cassettes and read and listen to them at home and then do a comprehension worksheet, in partnership with their parents. After reading two books and handing in the worksheets, pupils get a credit token for any book they want to buy from the class bookclub. There's also something called the 100% Club. When children get an A on a piece of work, they get a chance to guess how many sweets are in a huge jar. The winner gets a special prize.

The irony of the CIS classes in elementary schools is that a lot of children not at risk want to be a part of it because the activities are so interactive and so much fun. Says Patricia Norris:

> They don't realize it's dropout prevention. What they see is that we do fun things, go on outings, play games. We make things lively because the bottom line is that learning hasn't been fun for most of these kids. They haven't been successful or happy at school and it's my job to turn them around and to get them to want to succeed and stay in school.

One of the strengths of the CIS approach is its ability to identify specific needs and then go out and find a way of meeting them. As a broker of services and funding, it operates by locating providers of the services that are required and finding ways of funding them. For example, when a few schools expressed the need for an on-site social worker to deal with the large numbers of family problems children were grappling with, CIS went and found the funding from locally based businesses and then employed a social worker for those sites. Another school said that it needed a school counsellor full-time. Again, CIS was able to set that up and the school's literacy test scores have risen as a result.

Service Brokering

Here are some examples of other ways in which CIS has been able to bring services to schools:

CIS's partnership with Take Stock in Children is a scholarship/ mentoring programme that targets low income students in grades 4, 7 and 9. Each student and parent signs a performance contract promising that the child will stay in school, stay off drugs, get good grades and maintain good behaviour. The pay-off for fulfilling the contractual agreement is that the student will have her or his full tuition fees paid at a Florida state university.

The Boys Town Program trains teachers and administrators to work and communicate effectively with disruptive students. Particularly troublesome students are identified by a core team from the school and are referred to receive in-home support by a Boys Town counsellor. (Boys Town is a long established national charity working with children in underprivileged communities.)

Learning Through Education and Arts Partnership (LEAP) integrates arts into the daily classroom curriculum to make the the syllabus more accessible to all learners and to improve academic and social standards in schools. A recent project had LEAP bringing artists into an elementary school for a programme of study on the states of the union at the request of teachers who wanted to enliven the subject. The artists created a puppet show in which each child represented a different state, which they had to research for themselves. In schools where teachers don't have the time or energy to collaborate with each other, these residencies add a welcome and creative dimension. And by integrating the arts into the core curriculum, it's making academic subjects more accessible to non-academic children. LEAP also is involved in arts-based service learning, where children create artwork and crafts for disadvantaged children and adults in the community.

Focusing on strengths, not weaknesses

CIS's targeting of children is based on something called the School Success Profile, for which the Nike Foundation gave the organisation a grant to survey children's attitudes to relationships, peers, family, school and themselves. It's a questionnaire that is used to assess students' perceptions of their social and individual assets as a way of identifying risk factors. This asset-based focus is an accepted basis of intervention used within social services departments in the United States, but schools have been slow to take it up. According to CIS's secondary school resource coordinator, Pat Stanton, this is wrong-headed. 'We believe we can work more effectively by focusing on students' assets more than on their needs. We need to be thinking 'how can we make them blossom?" An education consultancy has developed materials designed to focus and develop assets of young people and their communities, which CIS uses as part of its support system to build up weaknesses which show up in the SSPs.

The asset principle is a central plank on which CIS is based. It's all about looking at the positive aspects of children's make-up – whether academic or physical or emotional – and using those as a vehicle to make them feel better about themselves, as teacher Patricia Norris did in the case of the 9 year old girl who couldn't read. It is only when children feel positive about themselves that they'll be in a position to take responsibility for their learning and acknowledge their own potential.

But the overarching principle of Communities in Schools is that schools are neither able to cope with the problematic behaviours that children are presenting in schools every day nor are they able to address the underlying roots of those problems on their own. When you have schools with sometimes up to 2,000 young people under one roof, all with their own dreams and nightmares, some of whom are able to sustain the many knocks of their lives and others whose resiliency has been knocked out of them, is it any wonder that so many fall through the cracks? How is one hard-pressed institution, staffed by people who are neither social workers nor psychologists and working with children who may be four or five years behind everybody else, supposed to make what they are doing relevant and comprehensible, let alone keep order?

As CIS sees it, schools shouldn't be expected to be all things to all children. But because of the unique position of schools as the common factor in children's lives, it's the ideal place on which to focus multi-agency work, providing social and emotional as well as academic support services. All those services are there, out in the community, waiting to be tapped by those who know how to work the system. All it needs is coordination. As Pat Stanton says, 'In the long run, with megalithic schools and enormous social needs within them, it's relationships within the community that are going to turn children's lives around'.

Whatever theoretical underpinnings are used, the theory and practice of Communities in Schools rests on identifying who needs what and then coordinating the appropriate services to reverse the downward spiral of those young people who have been labelled and categorised as no-hopers from the earliest ages. By identifying their strengths and their needs, by knowing the buttons to push that will have those needs met by the community and their costs borne by funders, the children of Palm Beach County are being empowered to claim their place in the sun.

Teen Outreach Programme, Roanoke, Virginia

It's been one of those nice surprises that don't come very often in the world of teenage pregnancy prevention. Over 20 years ago, Teen Outreach Programme (TOP) was developed to try to stem the overwhelming tide of teenage pregnancies in the United States, a phenomenon that puts the US at the top of the league in the industrialised world, with one million teen pregnancies a year: double the rate of Britain and triple that of Sweden.[1]

It started off as a small scale project in St Louis, Missouri originally working with at-risk girls. But with time, the programme grew and grew until today, it is a national organisation operating in thirty five cities around the US.

Its growth is due in no small measure to the fact that over the years, assessments and research studies have surprised analysts by showing that not only is the TOP approach effective in reducing teen pregnancy, but it has a similarly powerful impact on reducing school failure, disruptive behaviour, absenteeism and truancy, drug and alcohol use and youth crime. At-risk young people involved in the TOP programme are 11% less likely to fail courses, 60% less likely to drop out of school and 33% less likely to get pregnant than those in a comparable control group.

Learning through giving

At least as surprising is that it succeeds in reducing the incidence of teen pregnancy not through the vehicle of sex education but rather by a combination of (community) service learning and teaching the sorts of skills (conflict resolution, communication, decision-making, goal setting) that are part and parcel of good social development programmes such as that in New Haven.

Various permutations of community service or service learning are common in American schools. Many set a minimum number of hours before they are eligible to graduate. But what distinguishes community service from service learning is that it isn't just about volunteerism. Rather, it's

> ...a blending of community service and learning goals in such a way that both occur and are enriched by each other. Service learning projects emphasise both sets of outcomes – the service and the learning – and design activities accordingly... [and] always include a reflective component, where students utilise higher order thinking skills to make sense of and extend the formal learning from the service experience.[2]

There are three components to the effective service learning framework that should take place in the classroom. The first is preparation, which involves identifying and analysing the problem, selecting and planning the project and training and orientation. Next comes the service itself, which should be carried out in a way that's meaningful, that has academic integrity, that is under adequate supervision and that should provide for student ownership and be developmentally appropriate to the student. Following the activity itself is a period for critical reflection, a structured oppportunity for students to learn from their experiences through discussion, writing, reading, projects and the arts. Finally, the service learning experience must acknowledge students' contributions and provide closure to the activity when it comes to an end. This can be done through school assemblies, media coverage, certificates, parties and/or joint celebration with the recipients of the activity.[3]

To set up service learning programmes properly requires serious and concerted effort on the part of the community, with ongoing cooperation and collaboration with schools: it's no magic bullet. But when it's in place and running properly, it does appear magical in its ability to move mountains – otherwise known as recalcitrant, unresponsive, underachieving students – by 'simply' allowing them to give something back to the community and then building on those experiences back in the classroom.

Dr Joseph P. Allen, a psychologist at the University of Virginia who has evaluated TOP, is impressed not only with its efficacy but also with how its success flies in the face of so many other approaches:

The data not only shows the value of the Teen Outreach Programme, but suggests that intervention programmes that address the broad developmental tasks facing adolescents may be more effective than those focusing only on individual problem behaviours [such as early sexual activity]. It's a matter of improving self-esteem. And what we've learned is you can't build it by telling kids to care about themselves. What builds self-esteem is having kids actually accomplish something meaningful. To say 'Johnny, we all love you' isn't going to do very much for Johnny. But to have Johnny go do something useful for an old person in a nursing home – that's going to help Johnny.[4]

It stretches credibility to accept that something so straightforward could so dramatically change attitudes and performance. But the example of how this helper therapy phenomenon has impacted on one TOP participant, Howard Thomasson, reflects the experiences of many other formerly unpromising young people who are in the programme. Like the majority of TOP students, he is black.

Howard: 'scum' to some, a gift to others

Howard is one of those kids you become immediately aware of within seconds of him entering a room: 17 years old, larger than life in every sense, loud, attention-seeking, hyper. When the local TOP coordinator came to his school to talk about the programme to potential participants, he pulled her aside and said 'now I want to set the record straight from the start: I don't want you to expect good things from me. I'm not a goody goody and I'm really only doing this so I can go on field trips and get out of school'. Cheri Hartman gulped, took a deep breath and decided to wait and see how things panned out.

But then Dr Hartman, whose TOP programme in Roanoke, Virginia is one of the most highly acclaimed in the country, takes leaps of faith like other people take coffee breaks. And sure enough, like many before him and doubtless many more to come, Howard proved that this was a leap worth taking. Dr Hartman watched the transformation of a boy who some of his teachers regard as 'scum of the earth' according to a black teacher at his high school.

For his community work placement, Howard chose to work at a pre-school for mentally and physically disabled children. It was a challenging choice not suitable for every teenager: the children are demanding, there's a lot of mess and it's very physical, unrelenting interaction for 90 minutes. But what the coordinator saw, as I did for myself, was this great bear of a boy known in other contexts for creating chaos around him, sitting and making finger paintings with lurid green shaving cream with a couple of small children and then spending ages cleaning them up, gently sponging them down, all the while talking to them about what he was doing.

Earlier, he had pulled two little girls along in a toy wagon, singing with them (at the top of his lungs) and then tenderly helping them out of the wagon as if they were made of china. Sweating copiously in the afternoon heat, he was game for more fun, asking the girls 'y'all wanna go on the alligator ride?' while others stood wilting in the shade. This disruptive, sometimes EBD-seeming boy had become a warm, caring, infinitely patient young man whom all the young children clearly adored. His greatest accolade had come three weeks into his placement, when he overheard one of the pre-school teachers telling another staff member how lucky she felt to have him working in her class and how she thought he had a future working with disabled children.

Howard himself feels he is learning valuable lessons about who he is and how he behaves:

> Being in TOP, I see in the kids' eyes I'm like a role model to them. So I try to carry that along with me on a day to day basis, whether I'm in the TOP class or outside of it. I try to keep the same mentality that I have when I'm in TOP. I'm doing better in my classes and it opens my eyes a little more and lets me see what's going on around me.

He may appear macho as hell, with jeans baggy enough to fit another two Howards inside them, a walk that makes the ground tremble beneath his feet and a voice that could stop traffic, but Howard is planning to work with nursery children when he leaves high school.

Not all kids are extroverts like Howard and the programme accommodates those who would find working closely with other people more than they could realistically handle by offering a technology-related service learning experience. This involves students creating a website for a non-profit community agency. One student recently developed one for the local Alzheimer's Association.

Giving kids the chance to shine

Cheri Hartman is used to the 'magical' transformations she sees taking place in kids who grow through these kinds of experiences. An educational psychologist specialising in child development, she is the architect of Roanoke TOP, its coordinator and fundraiser. She explains the concept:

> There are many students in the school system struggling with the traditional way that academics are taught and who have had a history of failure by the time they get to high school. Many, because of having high energy levels or a strong degree of spontaneity, are seen as little more than distractions in the conventional classroom. We want to reverse the downward spiral we see so often, where failure begets frustration, low motivation, truancy and, as a result, where students believe less in themselves. By giving them the opportunity to shine out in their community, you see the successful experiences making them happier about themselves. And then you see their school attendance improve dramatically. That, in turn, impacts on grades. It actually reshapes their vision of the future in a profound way, helping them to make healthier decisions in all kinds of areas of their lives, from sexual behaviour to alcohol use.

Daneen Evans is an African American social worker and health educator whose professional work involves providing on-site health care services to schools. She's also among the army of volunteer professionals in the community who teaches (or, in TOP parlance, facilitates) the life skills curriculum in the TOP programme, fitting it into her work schedule and encouraging others from social services and specialist agencies to come on board. She told me:

> Because none of the facilitators are teachers, we run the TOP classes more like a group session than a didactic classroom. The children teach and support each other and express themselves in

ways that they can't in a normal classroom. How many other adults can they call by their first name? We don't judge them. And for students who have heard so many negative things about their destiny and who – especially the boys – experience so much tension with white teachers, our approach is teaching them healthy dynamics with adults.

Although not many people talk about it, race is an issue in Roanoke, a pretty town of 200,000 nestled in a valley surrounded by the Blue Ridge Mountains. While there is only a tiny Hispanic population in Roanoke, with a growing number of refugees from the Balkans and the Middle East, the black/white divide is there. Only two decades ago, there was still racial segregation in the southern state of Virginia. Today, black children are still being bussed into white suburban high schools, but racial mixing here – as in many other parts of the country – is seen as an outmoded legislated contrivance rather than as a normal part of life, and one that is systematically being overturned in one state after another. Much residential housing in Roanoke remains racially divided and when a black family moves into certain white areas, the all-American phenomenon of white flight kicks in pretty swiftly. Racism is not only a legacy in the south; it continues to be a defining feature of some communities, although not necessarily in Roanoke. Where it is an issue, you can be sure that schools, despite being in the frontline in the battle against racist attitudes, are not immune from it any more than any other sector of the community.

While the history of desegregation in schools across the United States has been by turns ugly and sad, in the state of Virginia it has been particularly shameful. Arguably its worst moment occurred in Prince Edward County in 1959, five years after the US Supreme Court's watershed Brown vs Board of Education decision to put an end to segregated schools. Then, white residents shut down all its public schools rather than agree to desegregate them. By the time the Supreme Court ordered the public schools reopened five years later, white parents had privately established a school for their own children. Since then, writes Virginian educationalist Forrest R. White in the education journal *Phi Delta Kappan*, various sleights of hand have been successfully instituted to keep black and white children separate in the public schools of the south.

Suddenly the race was on to rezone, rebuild and redevelop the cities in an all-out effort to create well-defined colour barriers between neighbourhoods, to isolate black populations, to demolish mixed-race areas, to relocate integrated schools and otherwise to create an even more segregated society than had existed before. (Brown vs Board of Education ruling)

As a result of ever more racially divided housing demographics based on northern models, 'southern schools are resegregating at the fastest rate since the Brown decision four decades ago'.[5]

Segregation beneath a veneer of equality

There are other ways that schools have managed to subvert the notion of racial integration. Across the United States, schools that have had it imposed upon them through legislation have adopted a clever modus operandi: a three-tier system that in effect creates a segregated substructure beneath a veneer of integration. It works like this: assessments for tracking or streaming ensure that the lowest achieving students are put into 'special classes' (J. Kozol, *Savage Inequalities*, HarperPerennial, 1992). These children are invariably poor and from ethnic minorities. The children testing average, overwhelmingly white and middle class, comprise the mainstream group while the highest achieving are put into the gifted and talented programme, which are also invariably white and often include academic high flying Asian and Japanese students. Every school district arranges things differently; but generally, while the gifted and talented students attend some mainstream classes, they have their own separate classes for particular subjects which may constitute the bulk of their schedule. At one well thought-of high suburban high school in the midwest that I visited in the mid 1990s, the gifted and talented group were predominately Asian with a couple of middle class white children. There, a very high achieving boy told me, 'We only ever see the other kids at lunchtimes and during gym class. Otherwise we don't have much contact with them at all.'

TOP is seen neither as an imposition nor a contrivance by schools and is even capable of breaking down the barriers between students and teachers. To ensure its school-friendliness, it has an advisory committee on which sit principals and teachers to ensure a genuine partnership between community and school. It seems to work. In Roanoke, TOP operates in two mainstream high schools, a middle school and an alternative high school by being invited by school principals to set up a class of referred or self-referred students. How it's run depends on the particular school. At one high school, it's presented as a course that any student may choose as an elective, receiving full credits on completion of the curricular and service learning components of the programme. But at the other schools, at-risk students are invited to join up for a year, with parents' permission. Most have a history of truanting, disruptive behaviour and withdrawing by the time they start high school. Half live below the poverty line. Of the 172 students enrolled in TOP this year, nearly 100 are African American. They are withdrawn from their main-stream classes once or twice a week, depending on the arrangements, for a ninety minute session which is alternately curricular-based and service learning, the latter taking them out to a placement of their choice. In addition to the schools, TOP runs modified programmes at a school for pregnant teens and a youth training centre.

Making community service relevant

The placement options – students can choose one of three or four – have been chosen by Cheri Hartman on the basis of their being inter-generational exchanges that are low risk. Working with pre-schoolers is particularly powerful because the young children look upon the TOP participants with admiration and something as near to unconditional love as some of them have ever received, and the little ones adore the extra attention. Another popular option, a nursing home for the elderly, was decided upon because the senior citizens relate to the teenagers' vulnerability while the at-risk students identify with the old people's disenfranchisement and being cut off from support structures. When you see a socially awkward 14 year old girl holding hands with a socially awkward woman in her late 70s, sometimes playing with the woman's wispy white hair as they chat about this and that, you begin to understand what these visits can mean. As that girl said to me later:

> When I first came here I thought it'd be gross and full of smells and stuff. But now I know what it's like and it makes me feel real good to think that the old people aren't having to just sit around feeling

bored and thinking that their life's ending. It makes me feel better knowing that we can make them feel better about themselves. It gives me a lot of self-esteem.

The aim of TOP is that the experiences the students gain on their community placements are processed back in school, rather than left behind. This is done in one of two ways and these are often combined. Discussion takes place within the TOP life skills curriculum, in which students are invited by their TOP facilitator to draw on their experiences and relate them to the areas they're focusing on, be it peer relations, anger management or negotiation skills. One example to illustrate this: a group of students working with young children witness a conflict in the playground, where two 4 year olds are having a row. When they come back to the classroom, they bring it up as part of the general discussion and the facilitator uses it as an opportunity to talk about what leads to and how to intervene in aggressive behaviour. The facilitator leads them into a discussion of how much easier it is to influence younger children than teenagers as a way of getting them to talk about the experiences of conflict they face. Says Lissy Runyon, public information officer for Roanoke City Public Schools, 'The community becomes a learning lab. You're sending kids out to do experiential work and you're bringing in experts to help them process those experiences.'

Another way of reflecting and learning from the community service experience is through the formal curriculum. The programme doesn't expect class teachers to know instinctively how to do this: it gives them intensive training on how to integrate the service learning into the subjects they teach. English has offered the strongest connections, so much so that some schools have embedded TOP within the English curriclum. Literature is used as a vehicle to get students thinking about their values, their identity, their contributions to society. At the same time, their community service experiences are brought into discussions to make the literature more relevant. I observed an English class where literature was the vehicle for reflection on life skills. The TOP curriculum was brought in to look at conflict resolution and anger management strategies via *Romeo and Juliet*. Students are asked to rescript and act out the key murder scenes as if Tybalt had succeeded in avoiding his murderous confrontation with Mercutio. 'Shakespeare turned over in his grave,' laughs Dr Hartman, 'but the literature became relevant and at the same time students were really reviewing and internalising what it means to rethink your anger and handle it in more appropriate ways.'

The principal of one school that uses TOP extensively in English classes says that he wants to broaden its use to include it within social studies; collecting the oral histories of people in the home for the elderly would fit in well and would have the added bonus of giving students' visits there more of a structure. The principal, Ray Williams, runs an alternative high school for children with learning and behaviour difficulties. There is no doubt in his mind of the power of service learning to change his students' behaviour:

> Every student here has failed in other schools, usually to do with structure and lack of self discipline. I've watched them involved in TOP activities and you see them as different people. They're taking responsibility for their behaviour. Having TOP here is filling a need in the curriculum that's not being met for these students anywhere else. They need every opportunity for social development. Our kids are experiencing less criminal activity than comparison groups, better attendance and an improvement in grades. Clearly, there's something they ain't doing properly in regular schools.

Which is precisely the point of TOP. While schools have a remit to deliver Family Life and Character Education, which encompass a broad-based personal, social and health education curriculum, the idea of a single teacher being able to handle such a multi-faceted programme is a myth, believes Cheri Hartman. 'That's where the school/community partnership is so powerful.' Luckily for her, the school district agrees about its value, particularly for non-traditional learners, and is prepared to allocate teacher time to the programme.

While nationally, TOP can cost as low as $100 per child when run by teen mentors, in Roanoke the costs are higher – $700 per child – because it provides services not offered by other programmes. Costs are met by private foundations, corporate donations and local government aid. Half of its funding comes from federal sources (40% from the Department of Health, 10% from the Department of Education), while the remainder comes from private local and national foundations and charities.

TOP Roanoke's added extras include after-school tutoring, which is done voluntarily by older students and retired people. It is also unique in offering a parent partnership programme. Once a month, Dr Hartman arranges family events where everything from inter-generational basketball tournaments to karaoke nights to guest speakers are laid on. The rationale is simple:

> We found when we started TOP ten years ago that the parents of at-risk kids were just as alienated from the school system as their children were. And from their perspective, you could understand why. The only time they hear from the school is when their kids are in trouble. So we decided to add a strong family outreach component to TOP. By involving parents, we can greatly expand our impact by building bridges between families and schools. With them on board, they're more likely to encourage kids to come to after-school tutoring sessions because we can explain what goes on and how important it is.

While at first it was hard to whip up interest, Hartman is now getting about 100 parents a month coming to have fun and learn a bit about how they can help their kids.

So impressed has the state of Virginia's education department been with the Roanoke model that it has asked Dr Hartman to set up similar programmes in other towns in the state. As a bridge-building exercise, it's labour and time intensive in the preliminary stages. Setting up the structures within participating schools, matching them with volunteers and organisations in the community and locating funders all takes ingenuity and diplomacy. But once it starts rolling, the programmes take on a momentum all of their own.

Not an easy option, but one that works

It's perfectly reasonable to ask what a programme in the Blue Ridge Mountains of Virginia has to do with Britain, the problems British schools face and the way things are run here. The first thing to remember is that TOP is replicated in 120 sites across the country, from small town Virginia to New York City, showing how adaptable it is to different communities. Just as important is the acknowledgement that young people in many countries around the world face the same kinds of problems, no matter what the social and economic circumstances of their communities. Like America, Britain's teenage pregnancy rate is high. Its record of getting children successfully through the education system is similarly unimpressive. The real questions are these: Does the will exist on the part of communities and the schools they serve to forge relationships in order to motivate children in totally new ways? Are schools and communities prepared to take a leap of faith, like Cheri Hartman does umpteen times a day, pursuing unconventional routes to get through to disaffected young people? Are educators prepared to see for themselves the way experiential learning can get through to the previously impenetrable, immovable child?

Quick fixes are not what TOP is about. It's too holistic in concept and practice and requires too much groundwork for it to be a simple, speedy solution. But the results show that in one year, children's attitudes, social and sexual behaviour and performance can be turned around. It's as if all these children have ever wanted – these kids who disrupt classes, who don't show up, who have been held back a class, who can't seem to get down to work, who bunk off continuously – is the chance to prove that they can do something of value and do it well. Whether it's trundling a wagonload of laughing toddlers around a playground or plaiting a lonely old woman's hair or using their computer expertise to design a website for a charity, the fact that they are being given the oppportunity to show that there is another, empathetic, generous, good-humoured, creative side to themselves seems to mean the difference between stasis and progress, hopelessness and aspiration.

References

1.   *USA Weekend*, September 26, 1997.
2.   Toole, J. and Toole, P. *Communities as Places of Learning*, US National Youth Leadership Council, 1992.
3.   Duckenfield, M. and Swanson, L. *Service Learning: Meeting the Needs of Youth at Risk*, National Dropout Prevention Centre, 1992.
4.   *Richmond Times-Dispatch*, October, 1997.
5.   Steinhorn, L. and Diggs-Brown, B. *By the Colour of Our Skin: The Illusion of Integration and the Reality of Race*, Dutton, 1999.

CHAPTER EIGHT

THE SEARCH FOR SOLUTIONS

'We must rediscover the distinction between hope and expectation.' Ivan Illich, *Deschooling Society.*

Over the years, the volume of material that has been written about stemming the tide of disaffection has been substantial. Researchers throughout the developed world have been ploughing years of time, energy and thought into looking at why it happens and to whom. Many more have been devising strategies for keeping kids in school, some of them contributing to a burgeoning industry based on marketing specially designed programmes that promise to be the answer to every school's problems.

It has become increasingly clear that there is no magic bullet or single strategy that is the answer to the varying degrees, causes and effects of children's inability to engage with schools. It is, rather, a combination of approaches, services, methodologies and systems that is likely to have the most impact. Whatever shape that combination takes, the one constant in the equation is that it must be meaningful and relevant to the pupils it is trying to reach.

The different models illustrated in this book are successful because the people who have developed them have taken risks in their own ways, going against the grain and custom-designing programmes that address the specific needs of their communities. Hostos Lincoln Academy's insistence on high academic performance in the midst of one of the poorest, most socially deprived neighbourhoods in the United States prompted a well-placed wonk at the education department to encourage the school's founders with these words: 'You'll fuck it up'. They didn't. Although it remains something of a curiosity in the alternative high school superintendency of New York, where academics tends to be superceded by choice and flexibility, the school has outshone other mainstream schools in New York in academic scores, attendance and extra-curricular achievements.

Hostos Lincoln eschewed flexibility in favour of high academic expectations. But flexibility is precisely what makes Jefferson County High School in Kentucky such a peculiarity, and such a successful peculiarity at that. Who ever heard of a three hour school day? Or a class without lessons? Well, in a town where a sizable proportion of young people have work or family commitments that make a six hour school day difficult to manage, the elegant simplicity of shrinking the day and individualising students' work takes the breath away. By paring the curriculum down to what the student needs to graduate – no more, no less – they are able to experience success and achieve their aims and continue juggling the various other commitments in their busy lives.

Clearly, these audacious plunges into the unknown were worth taking. You need look no further than their academic scores and staying on rates to see that. Though different in emphasis and structure, there are common denominators that they share, such as strong leadership and vision, well developed support structures for students, high expectations and coherent organisation.

The generic term for the route that Hostos Lincoln and Jefferson County took to achieve their aims is known as school restructuring, a buzzword that is coursing its way through the American education world like wildfire. Its genesis lies largely in response to an agenda-setting report commissioned by the US Secretary of Education back in 1983 entitled *A Nation at Risk*. The core of the report, expressed in a torrent of nationalistic rhetoric, is this:

> ...the educational foundations of our society are presently being eroded by a rising tide of mediocrity that threatens our very future as a Nation and a people. What was unimaginable a generation ago has begun to occur – others are matching and surpassing our educational attainments.[1]

Forget the bombast (this was, after all, the Reagan era) and what you have is a call to arms of the country's educationalists to wage battle against the downward trend that led to twenty three million American adults being functionally illiterate (40% of whom are from ethnic minorities) and nearly 40% of 17 year olds identified as lacking the very same higher order intellectual skills that employers today are demanding from their workforce. To add insult to injury, American students were international league table dunces in nineteen standardised academic tests.

So for the past 16 years, American educationalists have been struggling to find ways to not only get America back on top but to keep the most at risk children on track. They certainly haven't made it yet. Some would say they've still got a way to go to the first rung. But school restructuring is a way forward that has been embraced by many schools around the country in many different guises in an attempt to effect change. In its most basic form, it involves breaking conventions to find new ways of teachers, pupils and parents working together. A report by the Center on Organisation and Restructuring of Schools sets out the components common to all restructured schools:

- Site-based management and shared decision-making, with the school having meaningful authority over staffing, school programme and budget

- Students and teachers organised into teams responsible for most of students' instruction, with frequent common planning time for teachers

- Students participating in instructional or advisory groups

- Students grouped heterogeneously [in mixed ability groups] for instruction in the core subjects

- Enrolment based on student and parent choice rather than residential location.[2]

Interestingly, there are elements in the school restructuring approach that are the opposite of the way British education reform is moving. Parent choice is the exception, and we've seen how divisive and counter-productive it has been socially and educationally. Mixed ability teaching is probably the most controversial in British terms, particularly in light of the government's new Excellence in Cities initiative that allows high achieving students to be taken out of their schools altogether for fast-tracking classes. Where British comprehensives are moving into the realms of creating two tier structures under one roof in an attempt to hold on to middle class children, restructured schools in America are striving to find ways of meeting everyone's needs – to everyone's advantage.

Turning schools around by turning them inside out and upside down

There are many examples of school restructuring models currently attracting attention in the United States. A particularly innovative one that has lessons for Britain is the Talent Development High School programme. Designed by academics at CRESPAR, the Centre for Research on the Education of Students Placed at Risk, it combines research-based principles on student motivation and teacher commitment with specific organisational, curricular and social components designed to put them into practice.

Like the Hostos Lincoln and Jefferson County schools, the common core curriculum in the Talent Development High School model reflects the highest standards. All students take college preparatory courses: there is no tracking according to ability level as there is in mainstream (which is traditionally divided into college preparatory courses only for the high achievers, a general curriculum for the middle-of-the-roaders and vocational or business studies for the non-academic). Instead, all students take the same demanding courses.

Giving students real choices for their futures in the real world

So far, so good, but not so different from other schools attempting to raise standards and achievement. Where the real innovation comes is in the way that students are given the choice of one of several career themes through which they pursue their studies. In the 9th grade (the first year of high school), they are given counselling, attend talks about the options open to them and are helped to select a 'career academy' that they will attend. These are effectively schools within schools which tie curricular content to students' career aspirations from the tenth to twelfth grades. So while all students follow a common core curriculum at college preparatory (high) level in maths, English, science and humanities, they are delivered via the medium of their chosen career academy, which can be anything from Arts and Humanities to Engineering to Health. This means that the curriculum is no longer abstract but is presented with reference to actual problems and situations that students will encounter in the world of work. As programme directors James McPartland and Velma LaPoint put it, 'Courses that deal with real world problems and practical applications increase the intrinsic motivation of students in their schoolwork and provide learning activities in which students can get more personally and actively involved.'[3]

They also get more focused on what they're studying because the school day is reorganised to incorporate four rather than the traditional six or seven periods. This offers the possibility for more in-depth discussion and exploration of the subjects. And it gives more space for students and teachers to interact with each other.

Teacher/student relationships are central to the philosophy of this model. To avoid teachers being associated with the exam system, all exams are externally marked. Teachers' essential role is to coach their students. In addition and like the British form tutor, home room teachers stay with the same group for the four years of high school and act as advocates and advisers for their students when the situation calls for it.

Specialist help where and when it's needed

Another tier of support built into the infrastructure of the school features social workers, school psychologists and mental health professionals located on-site as full-time members of the school staff. For academic support for those falling behind, there is a peer tutoring programme, in which cooperative learning activities are built into regular classroom activities, as well as extra tutorial periods with teachers before and after school hours. And for pupils who have behavioural or emotional problems that keep them from functioning in the classroom, there is a PRU-type arrangement known as Twilight School held after hours which, along with basic academic studies, trains students in skills that will enable them to manage their behaviour. Students are referred there as a temporary measure, to help them regain their equilibrium before being reintegrated into the school.

When students play hookey, the school responds swiftly. Those who don't turn up for school are visited by a teacher who comes to their home offering support – not punishment – to the student directly, rather than communicating via the parent. This is an interesting departure from the way British schools deal with truanting, which is characterised by a punitive, not to say infantalising approach. By dealing directly with the students, teachers communicate the fact that they (the students) are being given responsibility for their own actions, and offer the support that they need to make school attendance more acceptable. Generally, once students begin their programme of work in the career academy of their choice in the tenth grade, truancy ceases to be a problem.

An example of restructuring: Patterson High

The programme directors of the Talent Development High School tell the story of one school that adopted their model. It's particularly apposite in the context of failing British schools' attempts to turn themselves around. In 1994, Patterson High School was declared 'eligible for reconstitution' by the Department of Education in Maryland, which is commensurate with being put on special measures by Ofsted. In an area with a high proportion of ethnic minority communities (60% African American, 30% white, 10% American Indian, Hispanic and Asian), it is what in Britain would be called a sink school, taking in all the children the nearby selective schools didn't want. It was considered one of the two worst high schools in Maryland. In other words, it was in as parlous a state as they come.

Everything about Patterson High was dysfunctional. Over 80% of students – four out of five – failed the 9th grade. Out of 600 students entering the 9th grade, less than a third graduated four years later. Truancy and lateness were so rife that strategies like issuing detentions for coming to class late couldn't be enforced because of sheer volume. In addition, small bands of disruptive students terrorised their peers and teachers alike. Teachers, not surprisingly, were on their knees with low morale.

It was against this dire backdrop that a collaboration between the school and CRESPAR researchers at Johns Hopkins University was set up in 1994 to create the country's first Talent Development High School. All ninth graders (first year high school students) attend classes in their own wing of the school building, taught by a teaching faculty divided into five teams. Every team has time built into each day to plan together and discuss issues.

Four career academies were set up for the tenth to twelfth graders, based on teachers' own professional interests and areas of expertise. They are: Arts and Humanities, Business and Finance, Sports Studies and Health/Wellness, and Transportation and Engineering Technology. Each academy has its own entrance and space within the building, its own staff and administrators.

In an evaluation of the programme undertaken a year after its introduction comparing findings with measurements taken the previous year, improvements – some of them dramatic – were found in school climate, attendance and achievement. The most startling turnaround was in teachers' perceptions of the learning climate of the school. Where the previous year, 80% of 9th grade and 86.7% of upper grade teachers thought the school's learning environment wasn't a productive one for most students, the following year, only 27% of 9th grade teachers and 4.5% of those in the upper grades believed that to be the case. Positive atittudes were consistently high in response to questions about students taking school seriously, teachers working together and standards of behaviour.

Attendance has improved, from an average of 71% over the previous three years to nearly 78%. Looking at it compared to other comprehensives in Baltimore, Patterson moved from the second worst in attendance to the second best. In terms of academic achievement, the biggest gains were to be seen in the 9th grade. Where only 47% of pupils earned promotion (meaning they attained at a level that allowed them to progress to the next year) the previous year, in the year after the programme was introduced, 69% were moving up a grade.

The creation and implementation of the Talent Development High School was a bold undertaking that may only have come to pass because the catastrophic consequences of not taking radical action were so clearly written on the graffiti-scrawled walls. It's not the answer to every school's problems. But clearly, this highly productive collaboration between educational researchers and practitioners has managed to hit on key points that other reforms haven't. The most crucial one is that when it comes to motivating reluctant learners, giving them choice and making those choices relevant to the world outside can move mountains. In a literal sense, the Talent Development model is giving young students a sense of their own future by allowing them to learn about it today.

What this and other programmes have shown is that a holistic approach to at-risk pupils is necessary if a significant impact is to be made on attitudes, behaviour and performance. Add-ons aren't the vehicles of change. Summer schools, behaviour management programmes and revised codes of practice are all helpful in themselves, but are not much more than damage limitation exercises or band-aids that you stick on a wound. To establish social inclusion in our education system requires more than that. We need to bite the bullet and be prepared to turn schools inside out and upside down, questioning everything from the scheduling of classes to the content of the curriculum, from how feedback is communicated to how discipline is enforced, from how successes are celebrated to how failures are handled. It requires intensive professional development to change attitudes as well as to learn pedagogic and behaviour management strategies.

Joined-up prevention

But even this isn't enough. If we are to tackle not only disaffection but the roots of it, we need to be looking at the problem more fundamentally, beyond social inclusion in schools. We need to be ploughing the right thinking, energy and resources into strategies that will prevent alienation and discouragement from developing in the first place. We need to be ensuring that children, from the earliest age, acquire the skills that will make them resilient in the face of the disappointments, failures, boredom, sadness, transitions and worse that they may experience in and out of school. We need to be equipping them, in other words, with the self-knowledge, confidence, interpersonal skills and emotional equilibrium to be able to navigate their way through life, no matter how imperfect the circumstances of their lives may be.

We've already seen how a holistically conceived and systematically delivered programme such as that adopted by the New Haven School District is not only raising achievement but instilling in pupils the self-confidence to resist the culture of crime, gangs, drugs, violence, failure and school truancy that permeates their community. Starting from the age of five and continuing, in various forms, throughout their schooling, children learn how to communicate their feelings, interact successfully with others, resolve conflicts peaceably, control their anger and negotiate their way through the many complex relationships in their lives today and tomorrow.

Reassessing priorities in the early years

The focus on social and emotional education at the earliest point of primary education in New Haven is paralleled in Britain with the introduction of the formal curriculum instead. British children are exposed to literacy and numeracy, as well as other taught subjects, earlier than children in most other countries in Europe, America and elsewhere. But, as has been clear for some time, it doesn't yield positive results. Recent research by the Gatsby Foundation shows that British children who start school at 4 and 5 do less well at reading and writing than children in Hungary, Switzerland, Belgium and Germany, where they start at 6 or 7. While an early start on building social and personal skills is shown to have an impact on academic achievement and social stability, learning to read and do number work early on does not.

Perhaps the next step in assessing how to improve children's academic and life chances will look critically at the pedagogic and psychological effects of introducing young children to literacy acquisition and the formal curriculum as a whole. That Britain is out of synch with most of Europe and the rest of the world should be reason enough to revisit policy. That our children test lower in literacy and numeracy than those in most other countries that start formal education later should be a cause for pressing concern.

There is another level to this preventive approach. Intervention that begins at the earliest possible point in the pre-school phase, such as Head Start and High/Scope, has proved that the sooner you start working with children, the more likely you are to nip problems in the bud by the time children start school. While both these programmes have been developed to address the needs of children coming from socially and economically disadvantaged families, there is nothing to say that young children from the wider population don't also have much to gain from similar programmes. As well as providing a pre-school environment for children who may not be getting the stimulus they need at home, the programmes have the added benefit of enhancing home-school connections.

Educating parents to educate their children

While both High/Scope and Head Start have been shown to have positive effects on children's academic and social development over a long period, there have been few assessments of parent training programmes. But recently, an evaluation of the influence of parent training programmes on pre-school children's behaviour was carried out by a psychologist from the University of Washington. There is evidence that certain ways that parents behave can transmit themselves to children, putting the children at risk of taking on aggressive behaviour patterns. Parents who are, say, overly critical or hostile or are inconsistent in their behaviour, veering between the punitive and lenient, or who are physically abusive are likely to have children who behave badly both at school and at home. In addition, their children often suffer lifelong relationship problems within the family as well as with teachers and peers.

In light of this evidence, Carolyn Webster-Stratton undertook a study to see whether working to develop good parenting skills with families of young children could reverse this trend. She worked with Head Start families because it is a programme primarily aimed at economically disadvantaged children, a group which runs a higher than average risk of developing behaviour disorders. She divided 400 Head Start parents into two groups. The experimental group attended a nine week programme which taught them positive discipline strategies and other parenting skills, including how to teach social skills and problem-solving to their under 5s. There was no instruction for the control group. In addition, a number of teachers and teachers' assistants were given a two day workshop on the methodologies covered in the parent-training course, to enable them to use the same strategies at school as the parents were using at home.

Dr Webster-Stratton found major improvements in both the parents' and children's behaviour in the experimental groups. The mothers showed a reduction in overly critical and punitive attitudes and behaviour towards their children, including physical abuse, and demonstrated more affectionate and maternal interactions. They also adopted positive disciplining devices like setting limits. In turn, children of the mothers who underwent the training were happier and better behaved than those in the control group. Best of all, the improved behaviour in parents and children was still there at an eighteen month follow up, although children were better behaved at home than at school. This was put down to the fact that teachers only had two days in which to learn the strategies, while parents had nine weeks in which to do so. But it represents an interesting reversal of the differentiation in behaviour before the study began, when many more children were acting out at home than in the classroom. What it would seem to indicate is that for teachers to have an impact on children's behaviour, they need in-depth training in behaviour management techniques. The idea of a half or full day inset session being the answer to a school's problems defies credibility.

The concept of early intervention is driving the British government's flagship Sure Start programme for under 3s, New Labour's ambitious new strategy that is looking to make its mark as a model of joined-up thinking in the crusade against social exclusion. While there are still many grey areas around implementation that are yet to be clarified, the general strategy is innovative for this country. Families with young children in 250 deprived areas will be targeted for support and advice on early education and health care over the next three years. They will be given guidance on basic interactions with their children, such as reading and playing and will have access to early screening and support for children with special needs. Outreach/early education workers will visit families in their homes and liaise with community health workers on the welfare of the whole family.[4]

Parent education programmes have a strong track record in Britain as well as in the United States and beyond. The Bristol Health Visitors' Scheme, Newpin and Home Start, among others, have been working with families of young children for years. The Sure Start idea has evolved from these models as well as from the American Parents as Teachers (PAT), a nation-wide programme – also adopted by six other countries – started in the early 1980s.

Parents as Teachers: early intervention for all

PAT is based on the premise that parents are children's most influential teachers and that they need help and guidance, no matter what their background, in understanding what their children need to be socially skilled and academically prepared for school. It has been lauded by Yale child psychologist Edward Zigler, founder of the Head Start scheme for disadvantaged children, as 'a vanguard programme. It's where the world ought to be going'. Another American authority on early childhood, Burton White, has said that PAT will 'revolutionise the way we educate our children'.[5] We may still be waiting for the revolution, but there is no doubt about Parents as Teachers' influence on the thinking around prevention and early intervention for at risk children.

PAT works by sending 'parent educators' from the local school district to regularly visit the homes of parents with children under the age of 3. There is no targeting involved: all parents are approached in maternity wards or at their older children's primary school. Those who voluntarily agree to take part in the programme are then usually visited once every two months over a period of five months, although this can be increased if necessary. During the visits, the parent educator will demonstrate how to read to and play with the child. All the while, she'll be chatting conversationally with the parent about how playing number games and manipulating different shapes and textures with their child will help its intellectual and physical development and improve the relationship between parent and child. It's all very low key, friendly and unpatronising.

A university educated mother of three young children who I observed in her home during a visit from parent-educator Evail Boyd in St Louis told me: 'Michael, who's 5, was always quiet and I didn't think anything was wrong till Evail first saw him when he was 3. She identified him as having developmental problems and arranged an assessment. So now he's attending pre-school special education. My regret is that I didn't start working with him earlier.' Her second child, too, has developmental problems that were detected at the children's centre that he attends.

If it wasn't for Evail working with him, he wouldn't be as advanced as he is now. I've seen such changes in him and I anticipate even bigger changes when he starts kindergarten. Watching what Evail does with the kids has given me ideas about what to do with them when we're on our own. Since we've been in the programme, I can see changes in them, in how they benefit and how I've benefited, too.

There are two great strengths of PAT. The gentle, non-judgmental 'instruction' on infant and child development and demonstration of the mechanics of creative play can set the tone for parent/child interaction from the beginning. Within the privacy of their own homes, parents learn from the parent educator how children need to throw tantrums and be contrary as a part of the separation process and how, rather than getting angry with the child, it makes more sense to distract them. She shows them how to enliven a child's curiosity, how to stimulate their hunger for stories, how playing with messy materials is important to their physical and intellectual development.

The second crucial point of the programme is how, as in the case of Michael, the parent educator can pick up developmental or physical problems early, allowing children to be referred to the specialist services they need quickly. In many cases, problems are dealt with and overcome before the child enters school. Speech and behaviour problems are particularly amenable to being reversed or, at the very least, minimised.

All this is particularly important in areas such as those in which Evail Boyd operates, where many mothers are single parents who live away from their own families and suffer social isolation. These factors conspire against mothers being able to learn from example by observing friends and family interacting with children. Another impressive attribute of the PAT programme is the sensitivity of the theory *and* practice. Just as in Britain, where working class mothers won't answer their doors to the meddling middle class social worker, African Americans are suspicious of white women coming to tell them what to do with their children. In the Normandy School District, where I spent the day with PAT outreach workers going out on visits, there had been initial disquiet among local, predominately black women who feared that these women were coming to take their babies away. But because all the parent educators are black and because the underlying concepts and methodologies of the programme were developed with knowledge and understanding of the culture that the families came from, the tone of the visits is informal and congenial. PAT has managed, through careful planning, to knock down the barriers between the professional outsiders and the communities that they serve.

The efficacy of the programme is undisputed. Four independent evaluations undertaken between 1985 and 1991 have shown that children participating in the PAT programme 'performed significantly higher than national norms in intellectual and language abilities and social development' by the time they started school. Furthermore, over half of those with developmental delays overcame them by the time they reached the age of 3. The progress shown at age 3 continued through until the end of first grade (age 6/7), putting them significantly ahead of their peers in reading and maths. Parents, too, demonstrated that PAT had long-term effects. Those in the programme were particularly involved in their children's schools and had a heightened understanding of child development and parenting practices.[6]

There are many other examples of preventive approaches that look at the whole child, although perhaps not quite as early as the PAT programme. And there are plenty of examples of good, joined-up thinking outside the United States that have lessons for British education action zones still on the drawing board.

The Centre for Educational Research and Innovation, a department in the Organisation for Economic Cooperation and Development (OECD), has done extensive research on member countries' approaches to young people at risk, looking at fourteen countries' policies and practices. *Coordinating Services for Children and Youth at Risk: A World View*[7] describes some innovative and effective multi-agency work that shares some features with programmes already discussed in this book and also offers some fresh ideas. The following three examples documented in the book, two from Australia and the third from the Netherlands, illustrate new ways of looking at how to both prevent and treat disaffection.

Lateral approaches to disadvantage in Melbourne

Collingwood College in Melbourne isn't a college at all but a small primary and secondary state school with a total pupil population of 780 children from socially and economically disadvantaged households.

Most are from non-English speaking backgrounds – Vietnamese, Greek, Turkish and African, some of them refugees. An inter-agency project, Extra Edge, operates from the school, linking up no fewer than twenty eight public and private organisations working in the areas of housing, health and welfare to bring their services to the children who need them. The project is run by three government departments, education, youth affairs and health and community services, but is co-ordinated by a group composed of representatives of the various agencies that includes the school's curriculum coordinator.

Extra Edge runs three programmes at Collingwood College that, combined, reflect its wide view of what it takes to mitigate the effects of disadvantage. Its programme for Vietnamese parents is aimed at preventing family breakdown, a problem in a community such as this where, among other things, family members' often long separations after dispersal from their home countries can create communication problems when they are reunited. Because of the complexity of the families' situations, project workers felt that a different way of delivering parent education was necessary. They were looking for a methodology that would be sensitive to the culture while at the same time offering to families insights into parent/child relationships that they could relate to their own circumstances. After a lot of discussion with the community, they came up with the idea of using Vietnamese opera as a vehicle to carry the messages of conflict resolution, the impact of cultural uprooting, etc. The opera was devised collaboratively, with parents, children and community leaders all having an input and working through the ideas, a process that was as therapeutic as it was artistically creative. The project has been considered successful by all the parties involved.

While such an approach wouldn't fit every situation, the power of drama projects to touch on highly sensitive issues by allowing participants to assume a position one step removed is well documented and can be profound. By adopting ficititious personae, the parents and their children were able to confront areas of conflict headlong, enabling them to look at their own behaviour and problems in a new light and seek ways of resolving them – all within a traditional artistic context that offered security and a link with their home culture.

Another Extra Edge programme is a peer education project for 15 to 19 year olds, which teams young drop-outs with peers who are at risk of dropping out. Those who have already left school are offered training on a course that will qualify them to work with at-risk youth, for which they are paid a small sum of money. It's based on the therapeutic helper concept. As witnessed in the Communities in Schools and IDRA Valued Youth programmes, the impact on the young mentor can be profound, raising not only self-esteem but also attainment and aspirations. And for the youth teetering on the edge who are being mentored, getting one to one attention from someone who has 'been there' is an inspired concept, showing them that while their difficulties may appear larger than life at the moment, nothing stays the same. There is life after disaffection.

The third programme is The Island, an alternative school that, since the 1980s, has catered for those who have either dropped out or been excluded. It's a unique collaboration between building workers and a 'visionary' educationalist who believed that these students need to be outside the pressures and structures of school to learn skills that will allow them to make something of themselves. Based in an old rough and ready warehouse, The Island accommodates up to twenty five 15 to 20 years olds who, while unacademic, like doing practical things. A team of 'instructors,' including a builder, carpenter, nutritionist, computer operator, jeweller, music teacher, physical education teacher and automotive engineer teach their particular trades and are supported by a coordinator and community care worker. After their instruction at The Island, all students go on to part or full-time apprenticeships or jobs and while only a few go back into mainstream school, their follow-up assessments indicate that they are no longer at significant risk after doing their training at The Island.

A model of coordination and collaboration in South Australia

Another programme, this time in South Australia, is based at Paralowie School, a school for 5 to 15 year olds which, like Collingwood College, has a high proportion of disadvantaged children including many from non-English speaking backgrounds.

With the recognition that the education system in South Australia was, because of cutbacks to other sectors, having to address many issues around pupils' health, mental health and social welfare, the school's principal worked to coordinate those services under the banner of what is called a Student Services Team. Its particular remit is preventing students from failing and dropping out. Working within this team, along with the principal himself, are three counsellors (two for secondary and one for primary aged pupils), a special needs coordinator, community liaison officer, a nurse, coordinator of the STAR Project (a nationwide dropout prevention programme) and the manager of a residential alternative education programme for older youth.

The focus of the counselling services is on preventive and developmental models of counselling. Central to its operation is the specially devised Kid Map, used by the Student Services Team to identify a range of known problem areas including self-esteem difficulties, lack of friends, eating disorders, withdrawn behaviour, etc. Through discussions with teachers and other staff, pupils who experience these difficulties are identified, then grouped together according to their problems and worked with in specially designed programmes within those groups. By grouping the pupils together rather than working with them individually, the young people are able to develop friendships and support networks amongst themselves, within the safe environment of the groups. Close tabs are kept on individuals' progress and as their circumstances change, the Kid Map keeps track of the changes.

As well as benefiting the targeted young people who have problems, the Kid Map strategy has helped to highlight issues affecting all pupils and has informed policies on, among other things, the personal, social and health education curriculum, staff development priorities and how school support resources are allocated.

Another programme run by the team, the Middle School Enterprise, is an alternative programme for disruptive boys. Based in the school, it allows them to attend certain classes but also offers them separate time and space in which to learn practical skills, led by their own interests. Some choose to learn how to repair or rehabilitate bicycles, others to play a musical instrument, still others to use computer programmes to improve literacy and numeracy. The scheme has made a significant impact on school attendance.

For girls, there is a separate programme. Analysis of the Kid Map showed up a group of girls in the 8th to 12th grades who were so troubled that they needed individualised attention to support them to stay in school. After interviewing them to assess their priorities, the STAR counsellor has considered it most effective to use a combination of individual and group methods, both of which focus on relationships, as well as referring to other agencies when necessary. In the group, the emphasis is on building peer support with other group members as well as on problem-solving and learning assertiveness. The counsellor also works with the girls to formulate their goals for their future career. To this end, she has started bringing successful women into the school to talk about women's choices. These women serve as positive role models not only for the girls in the group but for the whole school as well, raising girls' aspirations and at the same time the rest of the schools' consciousness about women in society.

Yet another strand to the Paralowie Student Services Team is the Salisbury Youth Annexe, a jointly funded residential programme for older youth heading for exclusion or dropping out. Twenty places are available for young people from Paralowie and a neighbouring school at The Annexe, which offers a vocational approach for youth at risk. Young people in the programme are taught skills that will help them run small businesses. The learning takes place through activities like restoring musical instruments, catering and bicycle repairs, with plans to start up a small farm in the offing. The aim of the project is simple and clear: to give these young people the housing they need, the skills they require and the motivation they are lacking to get them out of their despair/ disillusion/alienation and on track for employment.

In its conclusion on the South Australia models documented, the OECD report points out that one of the over-riding emphases that researchers found was:

> social justice for disadvantaged older youth who do not complete or are at risk of not completing secondary education. The equity, financial assistance, housing and targeted programmes of the Commonwealth Government provide a cushion to meet the basic needs of youth whose disadvantage stems from deprivation, discrimination, insensitivity of systems to cultural differences and other factors

beyond the control of youth themselves. The Commonwealth Government has the political sanction of the Australian people to co-ordinate education, training and employment policies concerned with national manpower and labour supply issues.

Within the multi-agency coordination of services under the auspices of the government's Youth Access Centre, it's up to the state and local statutory bodies to cooperate with public and private sectors to make things happen. What's particularly noteworthy is that

...the education sector has demonstrated leadership and commitment of major resources to sustaining services integration efforts. Within schools, there is a preference for education professionals to fill non-teaching positions focused upon service provision to at-risk youth. But South Australia is one place where the education sector clearly recognises its need for the services of other agencies and professions in order to keep some youth in school. [Its] Department of Education and Children's Services also sees curriculum innovation as essential to breaking down discriminatory racist and sexist attitudes, facilitating multicultural understanding and attaining social justice goals.[8]

South Australia may be a world away geographically, but its responsiveness to the multifarious and complex needs of its at-risk youth has lessons for Europe and America. The different levels of structures the government has set up to ensure coordination and collaboration of services reflects a vision extensive in breadth and deep in understanding of the issues and the ways they might be tackled.

Developing the head, the heart and the hands in Holland
In Holland, where a politician illustrated a similar understanding of the issues when she said, 'the problems of disadvantage enter society with the toddlers', a great emphasis is put on prevention. Rotterdam serves as a particualrly good example of joined-up planning, with its Fund for the Reduction of Educational Disadvantages (FAO) which brings together the local authority, education and social services. Its function is four-fold:

• to raise the attainment of at risk pupils by allocating earmarked resources to schools in the form of money or staff. Schools receive this extra allocation according to the proportion of ethnic minority pupils on the rolls, the numbers who are considered socio-economically disadvantaged and the total pupil population

- to facilitate the dissemination of ideas on how best to tackle disadvantage. Through evening meetings, seminars, conferences and regular newsletters and magazines, strategies and approaches are shared and discussed to allow a cross-fertilisation of good practice.

- to evaluate the effectiveness of policies and projects as well as pupils' results. Evaluation is a mandatory condition for receiving the extra resources

- to support existing projects and fund new ones that deal with pre-schoolers, Dutch as an additional language learners (including pre-schoolers), effective learning time, parent liaison and dropout reduction.

The effective learning time objective is the most interesting of the projects, modelled on the American Extended School Day. Specifically designed for at-risk children and youth, it offers activities during free time in the school day or after school that supplement the curriculum, all of them conceived and run by specialist teachers. A child welfare worker is part of the programme, acting in a liaison role between the specialist team and the pupils. Targeted at 8 to 12 year olds, the idea of it is to support learning as well as the creative and social development of the child. One of the workers put it succinctly when she said that education 'is not only a question of your head, but also of your heart and your hands'. So as well as literacy and numeracy work, children have a chance to engage in arts, environmental and sports activities – pastimes that they may be precluded from enjoying outside of school because of cultural or economic barriers.

In its present incarnation, the project is known as de Brede School (the broad school) and is constructed to allow each participating school to make adaptations relevant to its specific pupil population. Whatever variations exist, there is the common commitment to the idea that the fewer the differences between the ethos and experiences at school, at home and in the community, the greater the progress of children's development. And because of the enormous resources available to schools, it is there where the ultimate responsibility for creating educational opportunities lies.

Interestingly, the initially distrustful relationship between the departments of education and welfare has broken down as a result of the close collaboration on the FAO programmes. It is also the case that without the policy for educational deprivation being in the hands of the FAO, it wouldn't be possible to run so many programmes and to integrate them so successfully between education and welfare. To expect the two departments to cobble things together on their own would be unreasonable and frustrating for all the institutions concerned. As a model of cooperation, collaboration and coherence, Rotterdam has a lot going for it.

References

1. *A Nation at Risk*, National Commission on Excellence in Education, US Government Printing Office, 1983.

2. *Successful School Restructuring: A Report to the Public and Educators*, Centre on Organisation and Restructuring of Schools, University of Wisconsin, 1997.

3. McPartland, J. *et al*, *The Talent Development High School*, CRESPAR Website, August, 1997.

4. Ghouri, N. (April 23, 1999) 'Tackling the inheritance of failure,' *Times Educational Supplement*.

5. Klein, R. (June 5, 1998) 'Look Who's Talking,' *Times Educational Supplement*.

6. *ibid.*

7. *Coordinating Services for Children and Youth at Risk: A World View*, CERI, OECD, 1998.

8. *ibid.*

9. An account of the Brede School Project appears in Green, P., *Raising the Standard*, Trentham, 1999.

CHAPTER NINE
THE BIG PICTURE

Know yourself before you seek to know the children. They are not really 'children,' they are people; but with different understanding, with different gems of experience and different responses through their feelings. Janusz Korczak (1878-1942), doctor, author, pedagogue, children's rights ideologue, humanitarian.

What do we do with all the data we have? How do we process the sheer volume of findings, the diversity of approaches, the range of theories that define where we are today in the battle against disaffection? How can this mass of information and accumulated experience of good practice be consolidated so that we aren't constantly reinventing wheels and not only that, but claiming that the newest, shiniest wheel is the best? How do we assess what is truly effective and what is merely innovative? And how can governments most effectively capitalise on the expertise that already exists and build on it systematically, intelligently, creatively as an integral part of education policy?

Yet again, there are no easy answers or quick fixes to be conjured up. What we do know is that coordination and cooperation is necessary for change to happen on a big scale. We know that despite there being a great many initiatives in operation in this country, in the United States, Canada, in Europe and Australia, the huge tide of disaffection continues largely unabated. It is not that the initiatives in themselves are ineffective, but that the concepts and methodologies driving them aren't necessarily known outside the small corners in which they operate. With a few exceptions, innovations are happening in isolation and on a small scale, in particular schools, school districts or geographical areas. A fantastically successful programme such as Teen

Outreach in the United States or a holistic, preventive approach like Norma Redfearn's in Newcastle may not be known to the local authority or school district next door.

Similarly, the numerous government initiatives in Britain coming on the scene thick and fast from the Social Exclusion Unit and the Department for Education are by and large addressing specific aspects of the problem without really reflecting a connectedness of vision that makes for a coherent whole. Yes, let's have early prevention, working with families of targeted young children through Sure Start. Yes, what a good idea to give £40 a week to 16-18 year olds to lure them away from dead end jobs at MacDonald's back into education and training. Yes, let's introduce Pupil Support Plans to formalise behaviour management of difficult pupils. And yes, it's high time something like New Start was established to motivate young people at status zero back into learning. Looking at the big picture of Labour's policies, it is clear that the government is moving towards an ethos of respect and dignity for all children in ways that have never been seen before. And it is to be applauded and respected for that.

But there are crucial elements missing in the picture. First and foremost, there needs to be a bottom-up appraisal of how to lay the essential building blocks that will give all children a solid foundation from which they will be able to communicate, understand their feelings and learn. Hand in hand with that must come a developmentally constructed continuum of support that will see them through their compulsory schooling. Prevention is better than cure, particularly when you consider the devastating effects of allowing disaffection to take hold. It must begin from birth, it must be rooted in the community as well as in the family and schools. It must reach out to all children and parents, not just those who fit at-risk stereotypes. Resiliency is not the preserve of the white middle classes. Neither is lack of it the hallmark of everybody else.

The school as locus of the community

A fundamental place to start is the community, with the school as its centrepiece. Families, says theologian Martin Marty of the University of Chicago, have always been superceded by the 'tribe' as the most crucial guardian of cultural survival.[1] The tribe picks up the slack that exists and has always existed in nuclear families; it upholds values and standards. Many of today's families have become disjointed and the tribes/communities that have traditionally supported them aren't holding up much better – they're more likely to be on their knees in inner cities with widespread social deprivation and the demoralisation that comes with the territory. But despite that, there is much untapped energy and goodwill there to effect change. It's knowing where to tap and how to connect the different currents of energy that is the real trick. Schools are in a unique position to take the lead in uniting our contemporary tribes.

One community-based programme that has transplanted itself from the United States to Britain is based on the principle that the environments of community and school are locked in a symbiotic relationship. Communities that Care is a voluntary organisation that works interactively with disadvantaged neighbourhoods to help local people create positive relationships between young people and their families, schools and the agencies most likely to influence their progress. Underpinned by a melange of tried and tested theories and good practice, it uses a multi-agency approach to attempt to change the outlook of communities that have been dogged by crime, disillusion and hopelessness.

The basic principle is one of identifying the specific needs of the neighbourhood and then breaking down the barriers that exist between people and institutions and helping them to redefine their relationships. The aim is to tackle school dropout and failure, teen pregnancies, drug abuse and youth crime by working preventively to build up young people's resilience. It focuses on giving children oppportunities to be involved in their families and the wider community, on teaching social and learning skills in school and on ensuring that children's efforts are acknowledged and praised at school, in the community and in the home. At present, it has set up pilot projects in Coventry and Swansea and is hoping to spread to other areas. The programme is widely implemented in the United States, where it has federal government support. In Britain, it receives core funding from the Joseph Rowntree Foundation.

Communities that Care is a compelling example of a joined-up, preventive and therapeutic approach to the complex, multi-layered problem of disaffection running throughout a community. It's a positive and, hopefully, successful addition to the vast patchwork of good thinking and good practices that are currently cropping up with astounding frequency.

What it relies on, at its centre, are schools whose environments are healthy and productive, empowering and powerful enough to meet the challenges of its troubled young people and the wider community. In *Reclaiming Youth at Risk*, Brendtro *et al* outline the four major elements of 'the reclaiming environment' of schools: positive relationships with the young and discouraged; brain-friendly learning; engendering discipline for responsibility; and fostering pro-social values and behaviour, such as altruism.

The ascendancy of relationships

While some of these components may appear obvious to those engaged with school reform, they merit going over because they are so often overlooked in the scrum for control of the classroom and high attainment. Positive relationships with pupils are arguably the single most important factor in a school generally but especially so in terms of motivating the unmotivated and encouraging the discouraged. While the overwhelming majority of people go into the teaching profession because they genuinely like children and young people, that inclination can be subverted by the day to day grind of teaching large numbers of very different personalities and abilities big chunks of information in overcrowded conditions.

Teaching under pressure can push teachers into retreating behind a veneer of the controlling professional purely as a survival mechanism. After a while, that veneer becomes grafted on, like a second skin. And behind such tight fortifications, an attachment with children in the classroom becomes impossible. 'Many teachers find themselves teaching to spite the kids', says educational consultant, researcher and former headteacher Judy Larsen, 'not because they don't care about them but because of the raft of pressures they're working under'. It becomes harder and harder for them to reach out, empathise, try to understand. But without that personal engagement, pupils are unlikely to connect with the role model that teachers should be representing, the values they communicate implicitly or explicitly, the guidance they offer. In the most negative circumstances, they will feel that teachers don't respect them. And once that door is opened, disaffection is often just around the corner.

Hallmarks of a positive relationship include:

* *Being able to empathise with pupils, looking beyond the often unappealing, inscrutable or even forbidding surface in an attempt to fathom what is going on beneath it and responding to what you find.* When a child comes into school dishevelled and sullen, it requires a supreme effort of will on the part of a teacher with twenty nine others to worry about to take the time to find out what the problem is. But a few moments of compassion and concern can allow the child to express feelings and communicate problems that can't be shared with others. A Florida teacher told me about a boy who came into school in a rough state. It transpired, after she took time during lunchtime to sit with him, that it was because of having witnessed an incident of domestic violence at home the night before. He had no one else to turn to and if she hadn't put herself out for those few minutes, he would have continued to suffer in silence.

* *Being able to disengage from confrontations with pupils.* Every teacher will have experienced or witnessed a situation that has spiralled out of control because one person set up a confrontation from which it was impossible to retreat. Teachers have to remember that they are the ones in control but that control doesn't equal confrontational discipline. Allowing children a dignified resolution in a conflict by giving them the opportunity to make amends or apologise speaks louder than punitive recrimination. Compassion, again, can be all it takes. An Australian headteacher describes her way of dealing with potentially explosive situations. If a child says 'fuck off' to her, she disarms them with understanding. 'I'll say to them ' look, I know you didn't mean that because I know you don't really want to hurt me. Why don't you go cool off for a few minutes, take a walk around the corridor and think about what you said and what you really meant to say and then come back and we'll talk about it." The space offered to disentangle their feelings and regain composure is usually all it takes. Humour, if you can muster it, is another powerful vehicle for defusing emotional conflagrations.

- *Knowing how to earn the trust of pupils by being fair and honest.* Hell hath no fury like the adolescent who senses injustice. The child who feels picked upon by a teacher will, sure as night follows day, switch off from that lesson and, in the worst case scenario, bunk off. Consistency in the treatment of pupils is crucial. Just because a child acts out one day doesn't mean that they will do it the next. And beware staffroom gossip about the bad boy or girl who has misbehaved in other teachers' lessons: anticipating trouble is not fair. Children know when their bad reputation, rather than bad behaviour, gets them into hot water with teachers. And no teacher wants to face a class who corroborates the view of the child who insists that they are being victimised and/or punished for no good reason.

- *Taking the opportunity when it arises for 'life space interviews,' on the spot counselling/therapy/communication approach to help defuse specific incidents.* The Florida teacher who made a point of talking to the unhappy and unwashed boy is just one example. Impromptu mediation is another strategy that all good teachers employ many times a week without thinking about it: intervening in a conflict, listening coolly to both sides and offering suggestions for resolution. Not as easy as bellowing 'stop that now' by a long shot, but far more productive.

As well as positive relationships between teachers and pupils, the well-functioning school will ensure that other relationships within its walls are sound. Good staff relations are essential: without it, the curriculum suffers, the pupils suffer and, most of all, teachers are unhappy and senior management can't manage. Because of a compartmentalised curriculum, too many secondary schools are models of a non-bloody version of balkanisation: separate entities independent of each other, doing their own thing, labouring under mutual distrust and incomprehension.

Brain-friendly learning

One way that staff across departments can share pedagogic expertise is by motivating children through high expectations, affection and affording appropriate levels of independence. This is learning that is brain-friendly: it's interactive and experiential, social in the sense of pupils working together cooperatively, each taking responsibility for specific aspects of the assignment and in the process learning from each other. It is learning that promotes analysis, problem-solving and critical thinking. And it is the antithesis of that scourge of the secondary school classroom, the worksheet. Rather than every child for themselves, sitting and filling out sheets in silence, a brain-friendly lesson will have a practical component, perhaps incorporating role-play or an experiment or a physical activity to illustrate a point, together with a small group activity that involves cooperation, collaboration, communication and negotiation. You are assured of more noise and unpredictability than you would get from a worksheet-focused class, but the lessons learned are more likely to stay in the children's minds, as will the social skills that have gone into the learning process.

Discipline for responsibility

The third element, engendering discipline for responsibility, is about allowing children the autonomy that they need to learn self-discipline rather than having discipline imposed upon them. Autonomy and self-discipline are pre-requisites for emotional resiliency. A sense of autonomy is 'an internal locus of control where youth believe they are able to manage their lives and influence their environment' (Brendtro *et al, ibid*). We all know children who are held on such a tight rein that when adolescence hits, they rebel out of control. Giving a sense of autonomy in a school context, as in the home, means giving responsibility and freedom within clearly defined structures. The structure must be buttressed with rules, but rules that are flexible, not used as battering rams with which to punish the transgressor. The underlying discipline must be predicated on mutual respect. Giving ownership of school rules, guidelines, structures and procedures to pupils will help to encourage self-discipline. Children who not only know the rules but were involved in drawing them up are more likely to respect them – and can't complain about things not being fair when they are punished for infringing them.

Fostering pro-social behaviour and attitudes means appealing to what we know are children's and young people's innate sense of justice. By creating opportunities for genuine altruism and empathy, schools lay the groundwork for its pupils to grow into caring citizens of the future.

We've seen in the discussion of US programmes how service learning can turn children's lives around by giving them a sense of connectedness with their community and a feeling that their community service is valued. For many children, service learning will be the first opportunity they'll have had to redeem themselves in the eyes of the world, to prove their worth, to show that they're capable of taking the mantle of responsibility upon themselves and soaring with it.

Teaching altruism to the hardest-to-get-at kids

There are also numerous examples of how peer tutoring and mentoring can raise the self-esteem, motivation and achievement of young at risk people who are put into positions of responsibility. As Josie Supik of the Intercultural Development Research Association in San Antonio, Texas says, 'When we see children not as the problem but as the solution, many things become possible'. In the IDRA's cross-aged Valued Youth programme which operates in a number of cities across the United States, the results parallel those of the Communities in Schools programme in Palm Beach County.

At-risk students in the Valued Youth Programme serving as tutors and mentors to younger children improve their maths and reading scores, show a 20% drop in disciplinary referrals and stay in school 13% more than those not in the programme. These are 12 and 13 year olds who are known by their teachers as the throwaways. Louise Gaitanos, a teacher in the San Antonio programme told me:

> I've had other teachers come up and say to me 'you've got so and so going next door to the elementary school to work with the little ones? Are you crazy?' They are kids who were getting into trouble, had no goals, felt they were being pushed around. And then you give them a job that carries the responsibility for helping a younger child with their reading and when they walk into the classroom to collect them, the little one runs up and says 'you're here Mr or Miss Lopez!' and you can see in their eyes what a phenomenal thing it is for them to be valued and appreciated.

The notion of altruism and caring is high on the agenda of current American pedagogic thinking, particularly in the form of service learning. And it should be. The transformations it can bring about should make it a feature of all schools where there are children who are losing the plot – which means it should be in all schools. The skills that are to be accrued from these experiences are life skills, as essential to a productive and fulfilling life as knowing how to read and write. The Carnegie Council on Adolescent Development's vision of youth in the 21st century reflects this view in its recommendations:

> The young person will embrace many virtues such as courage, acceptance of responsibility, honesty, integrity, tolerance, appreciation of individual differences and caring about others. The young person will demonstrate all these values through sustained service to others.[2]

Bringing it all together

But the question that remains unanswered is how to move beyond the fragmentation of all these different strategies and ways of thinking to the point where a coherent picture emerges of what the priorities are and how they can best be achieved. While the NFER, the OECD and various academics plough vast time, energy and resources into valuable and enlightening research, their findings remain largely unseen by many educationalists. How can their work be better disseminated and how can schools and LEAs be encouraged to take up their ideas?

The answer may lie, again, in casting an eye towards America. The patchwork is more vast and unwieldy there than in Britain on one level, but because of that there are coordinated attempts to bring good practice together, too. Probably the best example is the National Dropout Prevention Center and Network based at Clemson University in South Carolina. It could well be a model for EU countries to follow.

The Center is an information clearinghouse on issues related to dropout prevention and school reform that has been going since 1986. It works with community and corporate leaders and education practitioners by giving guidance and offering expertise on training and resources. It is also a nationally recognised research centre containing a library and database and runs an excellent website for easy access information and data relevant to people working in the field.

Its function as a network came about in response to the need for practitioners to share information on at-risk youth and dropout prevention. It works by brokering services for practitioners and providing links between educators, communities, researchers, parents and the private sectors working in the field of dropout prevention. In addition to its research and information roles, the Centre runs national conferences and seminars throughout the year that bring together practitioners from around the country to share their expertise, ideas and practice. These events allow for a cross-fertilisation of ideas and practice that otherwise would not occur. Of course, they also serve as trade fairs, with the many different programmes, resource materials and consultants hawking their wares in what is an undeniably burgeoning industry. But the real *raison d'etre* of the events and the Network is to allow for the dissemination of information on a scale that means that people are being sent to the conferences from all over the United States and taking back suitcase loads of new ideas, contacts and resources to share in their own communities.

If this can happen in a vast country like the United States, why can't it happen in Britain or as a Europe-wide initiative? Until we can find a way of consolidating, sharing, evaluating and analysing the vast numbers of projects and programmes already in existence, we are likely to see a continuation of people spending huge amounts of time and trouble thinking about how to deal with problems for which solutions have already been found. Possibly by the people next door.

References

1. Brendtro, L. *et al. Reclaiming Youth at Risk: Our Hope for the Future*, National Educational Service, 1992.

2. *Turning Points: Preparing Youth for the 21st Century*, Carnegie Corporation of New York, 1989.

CHAPTER TEN
CONCLUSION

You want justice, but do you want to pay for it? (Bertolt Brecht,
The Caucasian Chalk Circle)

Over the years that I've been researching and writing about different ways of dealing with disaffection in schools in Britain and America, I've come across hundreds of young people who have been branded rejects of the education system. When I think of them, they seem for all the world like the Lost Boys in *Peter Pan*. A rag-taggle lot of boys *and* girls sometimes naughty, sometimes needing to break rules, sometimes perfectly ordinary except for the fact that they always seem to be looking for something else. However they express their disaffection, what they really really want in the end is security and understanding.

These lost, disaffected youth of sullen demeanour, angry gesture and few words are among the most vulnerable in our society. Whether pushed out or having dropped out by their own choosing, whether girls or boys, black or white, economically disadvantaged or relatively privileged, disruptive or withdrawn, from single parent or two parent families, academically bright or disabled by any one of a number of diagnosed or unacknowledged problems, they all have one thing in common: they're out of step – with school, with teachers, with other kids. Their difficulties may be transient or may be more entrenched, but however long they last, they're real – and it isn't fun. Being on the outside looking in is a lonely business.

There are as many reasons as there are gradations and expressions of feeling disengaged with school, as we've seen. Some are presented as external, others internal. Many young people cite a problem with one or more teachers as the reason for switching off school. Maybe the teacher is sarcastic or has it in for a particular kid – or maybe it's all in the head of the pupil. It doesn't matter, in a sense. Once the notion of a teacher lacking respect for a pupil takes hold, it requires a lot of working through to overcome. It's more time and energy, sadly, than many schools are willing to plough into an issue that pales into insignificance compared with other more pressing considerations – particularly if it involves a pupil who is typecast as 'trouble' and is unlikely to pay dividends in the test score stakes. So the conflict sits, festers and ultimately leads to the pupil either exploding or imploding. Either way, the consequences are dire.

Others will put all their problems down to a curriculum they describe as boring, either in part or as a whole. Beneath that well-worn criticism may lie an inability to grasp what is being taught because of literacy problems or conditions such as dyslexia or Attention Deficit/ Hyperactivity Disorder, two neurological conditions that continue to go undetected in many pupils. Or it can be down to a mismatch between learning and teaching styles. For the pupil with a logical/mathematical deficit, sitting through a geometry lesson will be like trying to follow a class in Ancient Greek taught by a Dalek. I know because I've been there. When you can't crack the code, you do one of three things: you behave in a disruptive manner, you withdraw into your own head or you don't show up at all. (Being eclectic in outlook, I took all three routes.) The same is true for the pupil who is primarily a bodily/kinesthetic learner, who learns best by moving around, interacting with others and engaging in hands-on learning. For these kids, the notion of sitting in one place and being talked at for fifty minutes is tantamount to torture. Of course you're going to act out when you're young and forced to do something so against your nature. Some children are better conformists than others. The disaffected haven't acquired that most over-rated of knacks.

For others, the social pressures of being in an institution where interactions with others are difficult can be too much to bear. Some may be bullied or teased, others ignored or ostracised because they're different. The child may suffer from low self-esteem that itself can spring from a number of different sources, including physical or verbal abuse at home or a recent bereavement or having to shoulder the burden of responsibiity for caring for sick or younger family members. Whatever the reason – and there are many others – the state of being victimised or being friendless or socially awkward makes school a living hell – and all the more so when the school is big, alienating, intimidating, when you don't feel safe and when there's no trusting adult you can talk to. When education is set in an alien, uncaring, unbending place, an environment that's meant for others but not for you, it's best avoided – if not physically, then mentally.

Then there are those pupils for whom school is just a distraction from other more pressing pursuits, like paid work or looking after their children. Often these things are set against the backdrop of a non-academic culture at home, where parents haven't managed to finish their own schooling. Their children's drift away from school, kicking in soon after starting secondary school, comes into play rather like a genetic *fait accompli*.

There is always a story behind the veneer of truancy, disruptiveness and disinterest. Given that almost all children start their school careers eager to please and responsive to learning, it's clear that for a significant minority of students (in some schools in the US, over half), something happens as they progress through the system to discourage them and throw them off track. Whether that something is to do with life outside school, within the school environment or, as is most likely the case, a combination of both, it will inevitably end in tears. While there's not a lot that education policy makers can do to change poverty and family difficulties, there is plenty that can be done to help children develop the resilience they'll need to face the vicissitudes of life, to motivate them to continue their studies and to have positive expectations of themselves and their future.

The series of snapshots I've offered in the preceding chapters have given glimpses of how schools can be differerent, transforming themselves into places that are more humane and less alienating, more relevant and less abstract, more challenging and less patronising. And more attuned to the huge panoply of experiences, cultures, perspectives and needs of the communities they serve.

What's needed is a consolidation of best tried-and-tested practices from a number of different sources, adapting them to fit in with local needs. It isn't easy but neither is it outside the realms of possibility.

More to the point, not to do so is no longer an option. If as a society we are determined to put an end to the wasted youth represented in the huge young underclass we've created, living on the margins and in the shadows at status zero, it's our schools that must be in the forefront of that campaign. They're in a unique position to build up self-esteem and give direction to young people who have had both knocked out of them.

The questions that all schools need to answer are these: If you were invited to create a school for the future, one that was socially inclusive in the fullest sense of the word, set in a mixed area that encompassed disadvantaged neighbourhoods where children were going to school with many complex problems, what would the essential components be? How would you engage the disengaged, motivate the unmotivated, raise the expectations of those for whom there have been expectations of nothing other than failure? How would you ensure social justice within the school community? How would you prioritise equal opportunities in all aspects of the school, from the curriculum and resources to training and staffing?

Looking at the salient features from the successful American models I've documented, what is clear is that without a holistic vision of the children, their problems, their learning and their communities, education reform is meaningless. To believe that, for instance, a strong behaviour policy, allied perhaps to a programme such as Assertive Discipline, can stem the tide of disaffection is tantamount to believing that one session of PE a week will keep children fit or that a half an hour of circle time a week will improve the school ethos. They are just small parts of the picture. Keeping children in line isn't what is going to change their attitudes from nihilistic to positive. Nor is it going to raise their achievement or make them spring out of bed every morning and skip to school with a song in their hearts. While a useful part of an overall strategy, behaviour policies on their own are more to do with social control than nurturing the desire to learn and succeed.

So, too, is the idea of creating more Pupil Referral Units, whether on or off site. While there are some, such as those documented in this book, doing excellent work with their pupils, for the most part PRUs are last-chance holding stations notable for low standards and low expectations. They are as inimical to social inclusion as special schools for children with Moderate Learning Difficulties. Their prime *raison d'etre* is to keep disruptive kids out of mainstream schools where they create havoc, interfere with other pupils' learning, drag down exam scores and put demands on resources that are better spent elsewhere. Ultimately, they confirm to the young people consigned to them that they're outcasts who will never fit into 'normal' society.

Sadly, there are no corners to be cut when an issue this complex is to be tackled. Certainly, the most successful schools and programmes I've seen have been those that have taken four essential steps. The first is to stand back and analyse what the problems are and the reasons that they've arisen. The second is to work out how to deal with those problems in a way that takes account of the whole child, informed by the understanding that school is just a part of the problem and a part of the young person's life. The third is to look at what strategies other schools have employed, how their evaluations look and how they might be improved and adapted for their own particular community. The fourth is to see how outside agencies can help to create a nurturing, supportive environment.

The recipe for a school that successfully challenges disaffection isn't a matter of mixing a bit of this in with a bit of that. Rather, it's about taking substantial blocks of practice that have been evaluated for their efficacy and that are based on sound pedagogic and social development theory and then fitting them together in a way that is complementary to and consistent with a holistic model of education. The ingredients don't have to be new, but each component has to have a proven successful track record to merit its existence. School reform to fight disaffection, like government policy, won't work if it's conceived as a melánge of add-ons, however of-the-moment it may be; it needs to be a coherent, bottom-up sum of its carefully considered parts. Here are some of the key ingredients.

- A commitment to restructuring, however lengthy, labour intensive and resource draining that may be in the short term. That means having the willingness to question conventions, traditions and home truths – and the courage to chuck out those that are inimical or irrelevant to a socially inclusive school. It means reworking priorities to ensure that children's emotional intelligence and social development are given the status that they require and the space in the curriculum that they need to be taught developmentally and systematically. It means a critical reassessment, for instance, of ability groupings and an evaluation of how they benefit or disempower children, especially those in the lower sets, informed by a review of the literature on the psychological effects of homogeneous grouping. It means seriously considering the possibility of reorganising the school day to create longer periods in which more varied work is carried out. It means redistributing pupils and staff so that classes are smaller and pupils are given a greater degree of continuity with teachers. It may also mean having to make uncomfortable decisions about staff who are unsympathetic to these changing priorities.

- Addressing the issue of institutional racism as set out most recently in the Macpherson Report. Looking at the overall figures of those who are excluded and underachieve, disaffection is, in part, a racial issue. Schools need to set up ethnic monitoring mechanisms to track achievement, attendance and temporary and permanent exclusions. Using their data, they need to evaluate their practices and see how they square with their equal oppportunities, anti-bullying and behaviour policies. Are certain groups being over-represented in temporary and permanent exclusion rates or other disciplinary measures? If so, what are the reasons for these trends? Is racist bullying a factor in black children fighting back and getting caught and punished? If and when Gypsy Traveller children enter the school, what is the nature of liaison with the LEA's Traveller Education Service? What support are newly arrived asylum seeking children given? Institutional racism is a whole school issue that requires everyone – from headteacher to lunch-time supervisors to classroom teachers and assistants to governors – coming together for structured discussions on issues around attitudes, behaviour and punishment.

- The determination to create an environment in which all students are valued and their accomplishments, however small, are acknowledged without being patronising. As was made so graphically clear from the shootings at Columbine High School outside

Denver, schools are liable to focus attention on a particular kind of achievement, such as sports, to the exclusion of other, quieter, perhaps less money-attracting ones, like art or drama or music or creative writing. But when an ethos is developed that says that all pupils, no matter what their abilities and no matter in what sphere, are given recognition for improvement, no matter how small, the self-esteem of all children and young people will benefit.

- The development of a behaviour policy that is fair yet firm. Clarity and consistency are the hallmarks of effective practice. When there is a mutually respected framework and procedure for dealing with unacceptable behaviour, there is less likelihood of pupils believing that teachers are victimising them or that other injustices have taken place. Behaviour contracts as part of or as an adjunct to individual education plans can be useful when regularly reviewed by teachers and pupils. So, too, is the rewarding of positive behaviour as the flipside for clearly defined sanctions for unacceptable behaviour. The nature of the rewards should be carefully chosen so that they're of real value to pupils and conferred in such a way as not to embarrass those who can't stand being in the limelight. Alternatives to exclusion must be devised, possibly involving withdrawal groups in which young people are given the opportunity to do a combination of academic work and experiential/vocational training with strong counselling input on-site.

- The creation of well-oiled pupil support mechanisms for young people floundering academically, persistently truanting or behaving in a disruptive manner. This requires a system of assessment and monitoring, as laid out in the Department for Education's Code of Practice and overseen by a special needs coordinator. Any support system that is effective has to be constructed on the acknowledgement that schools alone have neither the expertise, the resources nor the time to be everything to every pupil. Help to address children's social and emotional problems must come from outside and to make this happen, schools should act as the community base from which a multi-agency support team comprised of statutory and voluntary services is coordinated to address the multiple needs of the pupil population. There will be a variety of responses, depending on the nature of the need. Withdrawal groups for children with behaviour and/or cognitive problems is one approach. Another is intensive tutoring and/or group counselling before and after school. Yet another is the setting up of peer support and peer mentoring schemes. Properly planned and closely monitored community mentoring partnerships should also be developed. Particular attention should be paid to gender equity to ensure that while girls may be presenting problems in less obvious ways than boys, resources aren't distributed to reflect the view that 'boys will be boys and girls will be overlooked'.[1]

* A reworking of the curriculum that takes into account an awareness of the varied learning styles of pupils in any given class, described by Howard Gardner in *Multiple Intelligences* as musical, visual/ spatial, bodily/ kinesthetic, interpersonal and intrapersonal as well as the more traditionally academic verbal/linguistic and logical/ mathematical learners. This should inform a variation in teaching styles, so that classes are taught using different orientations. By applying the theory of multiple intelligences to teaching, pupils at risk are given enhanced opportunities to succeed, solve problems and communicate.

• A commitment to relating curricular work to the real world. 'The constant connection of schooled concepts and everyday concepts is basic to the process by which mature schooled thinkers understand the world,' according to CREDE, the Center for Research on Education, Diversity and Excellence.[2] It also makes academic study come alive with relevance and familiarity of the world pupils know. Part and parcel of this connection is to draw culturally meaningful contexts into the teaching, which not only excite interest but uses pupils' experience and knowledge to build on new understandings.

• A comprehensive approach to the specific needs and difficulties of ethnic minority young people, including appropriate levels of bilingual support to children with English as an additional language. It's important for everyone that the culturally diverse society we live in is reflected in the curriculum and in resources – but it's particularly so for young disaffected people from ethnic minorities, for whom this is a validation of their identity, history and experience. In addition, there needs to be an analysis of interactions between ethnic minority pupils and their (usually white) teachers. A CRESPAR research study looking at the role that non-verbal as well as verbal communication plays in the primary classroom shows, among other things, that African American children are particularly responsive to lessons in which group activities take place. It also indicates that teachers who attempt to instill a 'cult of quietness' are met with defiance and that teachers' mood and presentation skills are a critical factor in whether a class will run well or badly on any given day.[3]

• Teaching basic literacy and numeracy skills should continue at secondary level. This allows those pupils who haven't learned them at primary school to catch up before they reach the point of no return. Individualised computer programmes can be a powerful face-saving tool when used in conjunction with small groups. Hand in hand with this, literacy work should be much more responsive to research data on boys' reading preferences, which among many other things shows that non-fiction, humour, IT and action novels can make great inroads with the reluctant or developmentally delayed male reader.

* The adoption of an approach to education that encourages thinking and analytical skills through questioning and sharing ideas. CREDE supports the use of instructional conversation, a form of dialogue that is based on teachers' beliefs that pupils have much to bring to lessons beyond clear-cut answers. 'The adult listens carefully, makes guesses about students' intended meaning as needed and adjusts responses to assist the students' efforts.' Using instructional conversation transforms the traditional classroom which has the teacher in the role of interrogator and judge, into 'a community of learners...where teachers reduce the distance between themselves and their students by constructing lessons from common understandings of each others' experience and ideas, making teaching a warm, interpersonal and collaborative activity.'[4]

* A curriculum that prioritises service learning as an experience that positively influences achievement, behaviour and attendance. Rather than an added-on community service option, the most

effective approaches with the longest-term impact are those that integrate service learning into the curriculum. A number of studies have shown that those programmes that yield the most positive results are those in which pupils felt that 'they had greater autonomy and reponsiblity for their learning than usual, that there was greater support and collegiality in their relationships with adults in the programme than usual and there was a significant reflection component in the programme in which they read, wrote and/or talked about the meaning of the programme in their lives.'[5] Pupils who most benefit from the service learning experience in terms of self-esteem, improved attitudes towards school, better attendance and fewer behaviour problems tend to be at-risk youth. The contrast between their generally negative experiences at school and the opportunity to feel connected with and of value in the community sheds interesting light on the psychological effects of school on the young and vulnerable.

* Forging meaningful partnerships with parents. If it takes a village to raise a child, it takes a school to educate parents about the importance of their children's education and their role in it. Getting parents on board is one of the great challenges schools face in working with children whose school problems are likely to have serious ramifications at home and vice versa. Parents' own experiences of school may have been short and anything but sweet. Giving them guidance in how to take an active role in helping their children, whether with literacy or in terms of ensuring their attendance every day, can make all the difference between a reluctant pupil and one who's motivated to do well. Opening schools up to parents and community is a good way of breaking down initial barriers. Norma Redfearn's social entrepreneurialism in Newcastle led, as we've seen, to a school-based community centre being developed which offers a wide range of social and mental health services, classes and activities for parents. The result has been that parents have taken more active roles as volunteers and classroom assistants. By giving them a positive connection with the school, the parents have been more engaged with their children's learning.

* Last but certainly not least, a focus on social and emotional development in initial teacher training and a systematic and

ambitious programme of staff development in this area. Few teachers are equipped to cope with the challenges and the changes to conventional teaching that are being suggested. New schools, such as charter schools and some alternative schools in the United States, have the luxury of starting at ground zero with staff as well as with structure and curriculum. In Britain, too, schools within education action zones will have unprecedented freedom in some respects, if they choose to make use of it. Whether they take on specialist EBD teachers, counsellors and other child and adolescent mental health support staff remains to be seen. But whatever choices they make, for those schools and for all others, there is a desperate need to train teachers to embrace social inclusion with creativity, warmth and intellectual dynamism. They must learn the very best and most effective behaviour management strategies. They must also become attuned to the notion of a social and emotional development curriculum and acquire the necessary skills to teach it. They must have a conceptual framework to make sense of the strategies. And, perhaps most importantly, they must develop an empathetic professionalism that communicates caring and partnership with pupils.

The zeitgeist has never been more responsive to taking on and seeing through these huge challenges. Today, teetering on the brink of the new millennium, there are a constellation of possibilities out there waiting to be explored, tried and tested. Maybe it has taken getting to the stage where our backs are against the wall, where the sheer volume of the problems has forced us to look them in the face. Maybe it has taken a new government in Britain sweeping in, determined to make its mark by vigorously working to redress the excesses of educational, social and economic inequality that have been nurtured for nearly two decades.

However you choose to look at it, the time has come to embrace new thinking, methodologies and practices to bring marginalised and troubled young people out from the shadows and into school communities that are better geared to accommodate, care for and inspire them. Teaching young people who don't want to be taught can be the most thankless, frustrating task in the world. But when you transform the system, as the examples in this book have shown, so that school is a compelling place where children and young people can experience success and progress, where they can make connections that help them understand, where they feel they have a valuable contribution to make and where they are valued for being who they are, there's nothing quite like it. I've lost count of the number of teachers I've met, working in some of the ugliest buildings I've ever seen in some of the most run-down neighbourhoods on god's earth, who have said to me, 'this is the most rewarding job I could ever do'.

References

1. Hey, V. *et al.* 'Boys' underachievement, special needs practices and questions of equity' in *Failing Boys? Issues in Gender and Achievement, ibid.*

2. Tharp, R.G. *From At-Risk to Excellence: Principles for Practice,* ERIC Digest, October, 1997.

3. Newsletter Volume 2 of CRESPAR, the Center for Research on the Education of Students Placed at Risk, Johns Hopkins University and Howard University, September 1997.

4. *From At-Risk to Excellence, ibid.*

5. Study findings of Conrad and Hedin (1981) in Scales, P.C. *et al. Effects of Service Learning on Youth: What we know and what we need to know.*

INDEX